teach yourself ®

**baby names**

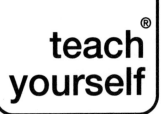

## baby names
victoria wilson

Launched in 1938, the **teach yourself** series grew rapidly in response to the world's wartime needs. Loved and trusted by over 50 million readers, the series has continued to respond to society's changing interests and passions and now, 70 years on, includes over 500 titles, from Arabic and Beekeeping to Yoga and Zulu. What would you like to learn?

be where you want to be with **teach yourself**

For UK order enquiries: please contact Bookpoint Ltd, 130 Milton Park, Abingdon, Oxon OX14 4SB. Telephone: +44 (0) 1235 827720. Fax: +44 (0) 1235 400454. Lines are open 09.00–17.00, Monday to Saturday, with a 24-hour message answering service. Details about our titles and how to order are available at www.teachyourself.co.uk

For USA order enquiries: please contact McGraw-Hill Customer Services, PO Box 545, Blacklick, OH 43004-0545, USA. Telephone: 1-800-722-4726. Fax: 1-614-755-5645.

For Canada order enquiries: please contact McGraw-Hill Ryerson Ltd, 300 Water St, Whitby, Ontario L1N 9B6, Canada. Telephone: 905 430 5000. Fax: 905 430 5020.

Long renowned as the authoritative source for self-guided learning – with more than 50 million copies sold worldwide – the **teach yourself** series includes over 500 titles in the fields of languages, crafts, hobbies, business, computing and education.

*British Library Cataloguing in Publication Data*: a catalogue record for this title is available from the British Library.

*Library of Congress Catalog Card Number:* on file.

First published in UK 2008 by Hodder Education, part of Hachette Livre UK, 338 Euston Road, London, NW1 3BH.

First published in US 2008 by The McGraw-Hill Companies, Inc.

This edition published 2008.

The **teach yourself** name is a registered trade mark of Hodder Headline.

Typeset by Transet Limited, Coventry, England.
Printed in Great Britain for Hodder Education, an Hachette Livre UK Company, 338 Euston Road, London NW1 3BH, by Cox & Wyman Ltd, Reading, Berkshire.

The publisher has used its best endeavours to ensure that the URLs for external websites referred to in this book are correct and active at the time of going to press. However, the publisher and the author have no responsibility for the websites and can make no guarantee that a site will remain live or that the content will remain relevant, decent or appropriate.

Hachette Livre UK's policy is to use papers that are natural, renewable and recyclable products and made from wood grown in sustainable forests. The logging and manufacturing processes are expected to conform to the environmental regulations of the country of origin.

Impression number    10 9 8 7 6 5 4 3 2 1
Year                 2012 2011 2010 2009 2008

**contents**

cknowledg ments

For my patient, supportive and grounded husband Adam, who certainly lives up to the meaning of his name.

# introduction

Whether the task of choosing a name for your new baby is something you find fun or frustrating, there are few parents who don't at some point feel a little daunted by the importance of the choice they're about to make. After all, this is a decision which will, in all probability, last a lifetime, and the impact it will have on your child is enormous.

The name you choose will become the essence of your child's identity. And whether you choose a name that is traditional, popular, old-fashioned or innovative, throughout your child's life, the name will inevitably cause others to make assumptions before they have even met.

Some names invite endless teasing in the playground or daily humiliation in the office, while others imply an elegance, confidence or sophistication which may be hard to live up to.

Perhaps the most important reason why this choice will be so important to your child, is that the name you choose now reflects a great deal about your feelings, hopes and aspirations for your baby as they arrive into the world.

For this reason, the story of how you came to choose your child's name will come to be very important to them later on in life.

For anyone who feels daunted, overwhelmed or simply bewildered at how to even begin making this decision, this book offers you thousands of names from around the world, broken down into simple lists that will help you find the one that you're looking for. And, to get you started there is also a short guide to the key things you should think about before you present your chosen name to your child, and set them on their way.

# 01

## the power of a name

**In this chapter you will learn:**

- the pros and cons of traditional and unusual names
- which names are associated with positive traits and success
- the rules about registering the birth and changing your baby's name.

What's in a name? You don't need a doctorate in psychology to be aware of just how much this one, simple decision will shape the way the world feels about your child, and, perhaps more importantly, how your child feels about him or herself.

Of course, one of the main difficulties in choosing your child's name is that you have no idea when you're cradling your newborn just what kind of a person he or she will turn out to be. It seems sensible that some cultures, for example, some Native American Indian tribes waited until a child 'came of age' before a permanent name was chosen which reflected the child's gifts and personality.

But when you choose a lifelong name for a babe in arms, what you're revealing to the world and your child, are your hopes, dreams, innermost feelings and aspirations about yourselves and about them.

It's little wonder that the way we come to feel about our name has huge implications for our self-esteem. Some studies show that a person who is happy with their first name is more likely have higher levels of self-confidence than someone who doesn't.

Other research reveals that a first name alone can influence everything from your chances of success in job applications and written homework, to how quickly you'll be accepted into a new group of friends.

# How to choose a name that will help your child

Whether a name is more well-known and traditional, or more innovative and unusual seems to have a very big influence on how other people react to that name, and there are pros and cons either way.

## Traditional names

### The pros

- Choose a traditional name, such as Sarah, Mark or Michael, and you can be pretty sure it won't date.
- The name is unlikely to cause too much teasing in the playground. Studies also show that we're more likely to be friendly and helpful to people with the same name as us.

- According to studies at the University of California, traditional names, such as James, Robert, Ann, Julie and Laura, also tend to be associated with lots of positive traits, such as cheerfulness and honesty for most people.

### The cons
- As traditional names are likely to be shared by others in your child's circle throughout life, this choice can make it harder for your offspring to be memorable and to make their mark in life.
- If your child has a very common name, they might feel that they are less special, or that you didn't put much thought into the name (regardless of how untrue this might be).

## Unusual names

### The pros
- Unconventional names will always help your child to stand out – people are more likely to remember them.
- The name you choose is also unlikely to be a fad, and your child won't be one of a wave of copycat names that reveals his or her age in years to come.
- It has become more fashionable for parents to choose unusual names, which means that children are less likely to resort to teasing just because of the name.
- An unusual name reveals to your child that you invested a lot of time and thought into choosing it.

### The cons
- Your child might stand out, but sometimes, for the wrong reason. For example, teachers tend to remember pupils with unusual names more often than those with common names. But while this may be beneficial if your child does well at school, the effect can be exaggerated negatively if your child has a tendency to misbehave in class.
- An unusual name is more likely to jar when your child grows up and chooses her own path in life. While Dolly may be adorable for your golden haired three-year-old, she may find it hard to introduce herself to the Board of Directors when she's 34.
- Some children can comfortably carry off a very unusual name, but others are just uncomfortable. It takes a very cool and confident boy to carry off Dude or Baldemar.

# Naming for success

Your child's unique talents and personality and your parenting and support are of course major elements in how your child will succeed in life. But you would be surprised just how much impact some names have when it comes to giving your offspring an instant advantage. Here are some tips:

- Research by Professor Albert Mehrabian at the University of California shows that James, Alexander and Charles are all good names for boys in terms of career success. Victoria and Katherine are good choices for girls.
- Men named Giles or Willie tend to be less successful than their peers. Alice, Bonnie and Sadie are less likely to enjoy career success too.
- How a name looks when it is written down is proven to have impact. Katherine, for example is more strongly associated with success than Catherine, because straight lines are seen as 'stronger' than curves.
- The longer the name, the more likely you will be thought of as honest and accomplished. Victoria is less likely to succeed in a job application if she writes Vicky on her CV. Shorter names, however, will help your child to be considered part of a team or group. Choosing a longer name, such as Robert or Jacqueline, that can be shortened gives the best of both worlds.
- Unconventional spellings, such as Suzee or Jayson, also tend to have the effect that a person isn't taken as seriously as someone who spells their name in the traditional way.
- Sexist it may be, but unisex names such as Ashley are associated with leadership for girls, but seen as more frivolous for boys.
- Consider how the first name sounds with the surname. Names with different numbers of syllables tend to have a better rhythm. Alliteration can also help a name to 'flow', but rhyming names can often sound like they come from a bad novel.

# Naming pitfalls

Before you finally put pen to paper at the register office, take a moment to consider the potential gaffes some parents make when choosing a name:

- Do the first and second names go together? (Mr and Mrs Curtain would have been well advised to check this one before naming their daughter Annette. As would Imma Hogg's parents – and yes, both names are real!)
- Make sure the initials don't spell anything unfortunate. Henrietta Anne Graham may be a lovely name, but your daughter might end up with HAG stamped on her luggage.
- Are there any common associations with the name that might affect how it's perceived? Will a son named Hannibal ever live down the memory of Sir Anthony Hopkins' cannibal character in the film 'The Silence of the Lambs'?
- Beware of obvious nicknames. Children are cruel and can often find something in even the most innocuous name to fuel teasing, but some names, for example those with unfortunate rhymes, positively invite taunts. Enis and Hank won't thank you on their first day at 'big' school.
- Is the name so difficult to pronounce that your child will rarely recognize her name being called out in the doctor's surgery?
- Will they be forced to continually repeat the correct spelling of their name – an issue which is more important than ever with the advent of email?
- Is the name overtly masculine or feminine? What seems wonderful now may be completely inappropriate to your child's career, temperament or physique in a few years' time.
- Is the name too childish? Can you imagine your child as an old man or lady with the name?
- Naming after a celebrity: Naming your child after someone renowned for their talent, beauty and success is a natural enough instinct, but beware: your beloved Scarlett or Orlando may suffer for your adulation. Not only do celebrity names tend to date quickly, but they rapidly become incredibly popular in all walks of life, including the less glamorous!

## The law and your baby's name

As parents, you are legally required to register your baby's name within 42 days (six weeks) of the birth in England, Wales and Northern Ireland, and within 21 days in Scotland. The hospital where you gave birth (or where the medical staff who assisted are affiliated) will notify the local register office about the birth.

Some hospitals have facilities for you to register the birth straight away; otherwise you will need to contact your local register office and you will usually need an appointment to go and fill out the paperwork in person.

## Who gets to pick the name?

It's usually only the parents of the child who can register the birth, and therefore make the final decision on the official name of their child. If the parents are unmarried, they may need a form stating paternity in order for the father to register the birth, or both must register the birth together – visit **www.gro.gov.uk** or contact your local register office, which will be listed in your phone book, as the rules vary depending on whether you live in England and Wales, Scotland or Northern Ireland.

## Are there any restrictions on what names can be chosen?

As long as there is no intent to defraud or deceive, at this stage, legally, you can call your child whatever you want. King Kevin, Sir Alan, Princess Tiaamii – although if you wish to change a name at a later stage, most deed poll companies refuse to accept names which imply the holder has a title that they have no right to.

## Can the name be changed?

Once you've put pen to paper, in England and Wales, you have another 12 months grace during which you can still go back and change the name. In Scotland you have up to two years to change your mind. After that, the birth certificate is a formal historical record. Technically speaking, you can still change your mind, and ask people to call a child by another name instead, but as far as official documents such as passports, medical records, tax documents etc. are concerned, your child will hold the name on that birth certificate.

If you miss the two-year window of opportunity to change the birth certificate in Scotland, you can still change it if you can prove, through documentary evidence, that the new name has been used for at least two years. In England or Wales, however, you'll need to change the name by deed poll or Statutory Declaration.

Once you've done this, the name bearer has a legal obligation to use only the new name and to insist others use the new name too. They must change their passport, driving licence and will need their deed poll certificate and their birth certificate for official purposes, such as proving any certificates like academic qualifications (which are in an older name) belong to one and the same person.

Of course, you or your child may choose to adopt a different name unofficially. This won't incur the wrath of the law as long as there is no intent to cheat or deceive people. It's a complicated business however, as official organizations like the bank, tax office and DVLA will use only the name on the birth certificate or deed poll. Decades after little Wendy has become known to the world as Anne, she'll still baffle the postman with the large quantities of mail which arrive in her official name.

## If you lose your baby

No one likes to think about the possibility, but in the tragic event that you should lose your baby, choosing a name is important too. Not only does it give your little one the dignity that comes with a name, but it can help you as parents through the grieving process, because you are acknowledging the baby as a person. If you miscarried early and do not know the sex of the child, you may have a strong inner sense of whether your child was a boy or a girl. If not, you could try using a name which suits either sex.

Whatever your decision, it's important that you have as much support as possible during this difficult time. The Miscarriage Association offers comfort and advice for those who have lost a baby during pregnancy. For more information, see their website at **www.miscarriageassociation.org.uk** or call their helpline on 01924 200799. Those whose babies were stillborn, or who died soon after birth (no matter how long ago) may wish to contact the Stillbirth and Neonatal Death Society. Their website is **www.uk-sands.org** and their helpline is 020 7436 5881.

# Your baby-naming checklist

- How does your baby's full name sound? Try saying it aloud a few times in different contexts to see if it's a tongue-twister or likely to be horribly inappropriate in some contexts. 'Tabitha Tibbetson? Have you got your PE kit?' or 'Hello, my name is Tinkerbell Jones and I'm here as counsel for the defence...'
- What do the initials spell?
- Can people pronounce it easily?
- Can people spell it easily?
- Are there any obvious horrible nicknames? How playground-proof is it?
- Have you looked up the meaning? It might not matter to you, but just double-check so you're not too upset when you find out that your daughter Rebecca's names mean heifer in Hebrew.
- What might the name be shortened to, and do you like that?
- Is it possible that the name might be wildly inappropriate to your child's character or physique?
- Do you *love* it?

# 02

## baby-naming etiquette

**In this chapter you will learn:**
- the rules and traditions concerning middle names
- all the options for choosing your child's surname
- how to avoid common baby naming gaffes.

Your child's name should ultimately be your choice, regardless of tradition, the sentiment of friends or family and what's generally considered 'the done thing'. But it's a choice which will have an impact not just on you but on your family and all of those who have to use the name frequently throughout your baby's life. There is often sound reasoning behind some of the long-standing traditions and etiquette surrounding naming which can help you avoid resentful or awkward sentiments being attached to the word that will come to represent your child.

## If you can't agree on a name

If you and your partner have your hearts set on very different names, or you simply can't find one that you both like, you could try these ways to settle the matter:

- Mum chooses a girl's name and Dad gets to choose the boy's name. If one of you utterly loathes the name your partner has chosen for one gender, do it the other way around.
- Do the names you've chosen blend into another? Could Lily and Elizabeth be Lilabeth? Or John and Adrian be Jaydon?
- Give your child both names; one as a first name, one as a middle name, so later in life they can choose to go by their middle name if they prefer.
- If you each prefer a different name, test them both methodically. Search the internet to find out how popular they are, ask friends and family their thoughts and check meanings. Then sit down and write a lit of pros and cons for each name.
- Get to the heart of what you're both looking for in a name to work out a compromise. If one of you believes a traditional, timeless name is best, and the other is searching for uniqueness and individuality, could you perhaps use a traditional name with a less common spelling or use a longer name with an unusual shortened version so your child can get the best of both worlds?

## When to name your baby

Nowadays when parents often know the sex of the baby at the 20-week scan, some parents feel it appropriate to name their baby at this point. Yet there are good reasons why tradition and etiquette dictate that parents wait until their baby arrives before announcing to the world the name they have set their hearts on.

Firstly, it gives relatives and friends no time to argue about the name and try to change your mind. Also, if you do change your mind and come across a name you love much better, you can do so without any fuss. Announcing the name at the birth also means that you'll naturally reveal the name in an appropriate pecking order, those closest to you will know it first. It's also worth bearing in mind that while scans are accurate for the most part, your son, Jezabelle may not live it down if the radiographer has made a mistake.

Mainly though, saving your announcement of the name until the actual announcement of birth gives the moment a special significance. Also, many parents change their mind on seeing their newborn for the first time. The tiny little girl clinging to her mother's finger just might not 'look like an Olivia'. Your instincts can help you find a name that fits.

## Name-stealing: a modern-day crime

The recent trend for choosing unusual and creative names for children has led to a new 'crime' when it comes to baby-naming etiquette. Name-stealing, where a friend or relative deliberately chooses a name which you've picked out for your own unborn child, has become a modern-day faux pas. It's only natural that someone will feel outraged if you mix in the same circles and use the same name that they were openly planning to use for their own child. But there are varying degrees to this crime. While you might be forgiven for using a name which has made the top 100 list of most popular names, using the name that your unmarried best friend has set her heart on is a little harder to defend if she's made it up herself. Likewise, if you use the name that your pregnant friend and her partner have spent many hours deciding on, it's much more inappropriate than using a name that your single friend, who has no plans for children, has vaguely mentioned along with several other possible choices. And if a name happens to have special emotional significance to you, as the name of a much-loved aunt who's passed away for example, the matter of who got there first simply becomes trivial.

# Naming your baby after a family member

There's no doubt that naming your baby after someone is a moving and lasting tribute. The tradition of naming children after family members dates back to Medieval times. Not only does this choice reveal how important your family is to you, but it can encourage a bond between your child and their namesake, or give a sense of commemoration and continuity if you use the name of a loved one who has passed away.

It might be the case, however, that a family member expects you to use a name you simply hate. In this instance you could get around the problem by using a different version of the name, or a different part of Grandma's name – like her maiden name, for example. If you can't find a harmonious solution, ultimately you have to decide if it's worth making your child carry the name simply to save your relative's feelings.

# Middle names

The use of middle names did not start in Britain until the seventeenth century when the aristocracy began the practice. But the fashion trickled down through the class system and remains so popular today that it's considered unusual not to have one. There are several good reasons for choosing a middle name for your child.

- A middle name is an excellent way to give your child a family member's name without it imposing on their individual identity or burdening them with an embarrassing or dated first name.
- If a mother wants to carry on her family name but a child will carry the father's surname, the mother's maiden name can be used as a middle name.
- Sometimes a middle name can take on religious significance. For example, Catholics may use a confirmation name as a middle name, or the middle name may be that of a particular saint.
- The middle name is a second chance and a safety net. You give your child a second option, which it's easy for them to switch to in later life. It's common for people to go by their middle name and it's easy to establish identity for official purposes if the name you are going by appears on your official documents as your middle name.

- It's also handy for those times in life when you would prefer to use a pseudonym. An author choosing a pen name, for example.

There are no legal requirements to give your child a middle name, however, and the number of middle names you choose is up to you too. Not giving your child a middle name might make form-filling easier, and avoid the prospect of an embarrassing middle name. On the other hand, it will give them fewer options in what name they wish to go by in later life, and they may feel as though they are lacking something which you could have easily given them.

Choosing too many middle names will make any official applications something of a nightmare, and unless you are a member of the nobility, a long list of names along the lines of James Wilberforth George Arthur Parker could suggest you are trying to give that impression! Either that, or you really couldn't come to any clear decision.

## When must you use your middle name?

Full given names must be used in the following situations:

- When applying for a passport.
- When applying for a bank account.
- When applying for a driving licence.
- During a marriage ceremony.
- During court proceedings.

## How to choose a good middle name:

- Make sure it sounds good aloud. As a general rule, longer middle names work best with shorter first names and vice versa.
- Avoid middle names that rhyme with the first or last name.
- Try to avoid syllables that repeat next to each other in the name. For example: Karen Renata Brown or Julie Leanne Hamilton. They make terrible tongue-twisters.
- If you've chosen an original and creative first name, give your child the option of a more conventional middle name. They can always make a more traditional first name their own in other ways, by changing spelling or pronunciation or by using an unusual nickname, but if Moonflower turns out to be a boardroom tiger rather than a eco-inspired artist, she may prefer Teresa to Trixie as a middle name.

# Surnames

It hasn't always been the unquestioned tradition that children carry their father's surnames. Historically, it has been traditional for children to carry their mother's name if she was wealthier or from a more noble family than her husband.

Nowadays, the tradition of the child automatically inheriting the father's surname is changing once again and so it's likely many families will have to make a conscious choice at this point about which last name their child is going to carry.

It's now more common for both mother and father to keep their original surnames, or for parents to remarry. It is also more common for parents *not* to be married and so still have their own surnames. In these circumstances, there are a few options available to you:

- Use a double-barrelled name.
- A trend that's becoming popular in the US is to mesh names so you use part of both surnames to form a completely new one. Carpenter and Wilton, for example could become Carlton.
- One more choice is to use one parent's family name as a middle name. Names like Wilson and Jackson have recently become more popular partly because of this trend.

## Tips for using a double-barrelled name

- Decide whether you're going to use a hyphen or not. If you don't then, in general use, your child's name will just be the last part of the surname. For example, while the birth certificate may say Rebecca Jane Green Smith, your daughter will receive letters to Rebecca Smith.
- Whose name goes first? Traditionally the man's surname goes last, but many couples prefer to decide based on which version sounds better.
- As a rule, names with a different number of syllables and which don't rhyme sound best together.

# 03 predicting trends

**In this chapter you will learn:**
- which names have been popular in recent years
- key trends in baby naming
- how to choose a timeless name.

It's important when you're making your decision to at least be aware of trends in baby-naming, because regardless of whether you want to make sure the name is in vogue or you simply don't care, the changing fads will have an impact on how your baby's name is perceived by others.

Think of Ethel, Albert or Wilfred for example, and it's pretty likely that you're thinking of an older person. You might adore the name Chardonnay, but thanks to the power of TV and baby-naming fashions, the name has connotations which are more 'Footballer's Wives' than fine wine.

Here's an outline of how baby-naming fashions tend to affect the way people react to names and how to predict the impact they will have on the name you eventually choose.

# Current trends

If you were to look at the current list of most popular baby names, you'll see three or four key trends in choosing names at the moment.

## Old-fashioned names

In 2007, Grace, Ruby and Olivia were the top three most popular names, with Millie and Evie in the top 30, revealing that names that were previously thought old-fashioned are now back in vogue. Just as in the world of fashion, fads run in cycles and it currently seems as if names that were popular at the beginning of the century are now the latest hit at the register office.

Although Thomas is something of a perennial favourite, Joshua and Jack have been in the top five names consistently for the last five years, with even more traditionally old-fashioned names such as Alfie and Archie making the top 50 in 2007.

### *The pros*

The fact that names which were popular in our grandparents' youth are no longer seen as dated is wonderful in many ways. There's something adorable in your beautiful daughter carrying a name such as Dora which has lasted for so many generations, almost like handing down a beautiful, long-forgotten family heirloom. And of course, it's so much easier to give a name which will be a heart-warming tribute to an older relative.

There's also the argument that if a name has such a long-standing history, then it will stand the test of time once again.

## The cons

No doubt many of the parents of the 1970s believed that giving their children old-fashioned names (some of which were also shortened for fashionable effect) was a recipe for giving them respectable, unusual and timeless names. Yet a generation of Sharons, Vickys and Garys now reveal their age almost as surely as if they had handed you their date of birth when they tell you their name. Because these particular names became incredibly popular very quickly, they remained cool for about as long as fluffy dice did. Some of the classic style of an old-fashioned name is undermined simply by the fact that so many others follow suit.

## Celebrity names

In an age where celebrity has never been more powerful, it's perhaps not surprising that names such as Keira (Knightly, actress) and Scarlett (Johannson, actress) along with Leona (Lewis, X Factor winner) and Theo (Walcott, footballer) shoot up the baby name league tables in tandem with the rising fame of the stars who brought the name to public notice.

The often bizarre names of celebrities' children also inspire many parents. David and Victoria Beckham's youngest son's name, Cruz, rose in popularity by 245 per cent between 2005 and 2006. Ava, the daughter of singer and presenter Myleene Klass, rose 23 places last year.

### The pros

Naming children after celebrities may seem to be a recent trend but it's happened throughout the ages. Ingrid Bergman inspired a host of namesakes in the 1930s and, going back even further, William only became popular after William the Conqueror arrived in 1066. The main benefit, of course, is that the name will always carry some of the kudos associated with the celebrity.

### The cons

If a celebrity happens to stay popular for a long time, then the name can remain fashionable and cool for years to come. Sometimes the name even becomes so perennially popular that it becomes relatively timeless. However, fame is often fleeting and the name's popularity is liable to wane as the lights go down. Celebrity-inspired names are notorious for going out of date quickly and also for quickly gaining 'chav' status. What at first might seem to be the unusual and fashionable name of the moment, can quickly seem more bargain basement than designer cool.

# Most popular baby names: 2003 to 2007

[Source: *Office of National Statistics*]

[Key: =* means of equal rank/popularity]

## Boys

|    | 2003 | 2004 | 2005 | 2006 | 2007 |
|----|------|------|------|------|------|
| 1 | JACK | JACK | JACK | JACK | JACK |
| 2 | JOSHUA | JOSHUA | JOSHUA | THOMAS | THOMAS |
| 3 | THOMAS | THOMAS | THOMAS | JOSHUA | OLIVER |
| 4 | JAMES | JAMES | JAMES | OLIVER | JOSHUA |
| 5 | DANIEL | DANIEL | OLIVER | HARRY | HARRY |
| 6 | OLIVER | SAMUEL | DANIEL | JAMES | CHARLIE |
| 7 | BENJAMIN | OLIVER | SAMUEL | WILLIAM | DANIEL |
| 8 | SAMUEL | WILLIAM | WILLIAM | SAMUEL | WILLIAM |
| 9 | WILLIAM | BENJAMIN | HARRY | DANIEL | JAMES |
| 10 | JOSEPH | JOSEPH | JOSEPH | CHARLIE | ALFIE |
| 11 | HARRY | HARRY | BENJAMIN | BENJAMIN | SAMUEL |
| 12 | MATTHEW | MATTHEW | CHARLIE | JOSEPH | GEORGE |
| 13 | LEWIS | LEWIS | LUKE | CALLUM | JOSEPH |
| 14 | LUKE | ETHAN | MATTHEW | GEORGE | BENJAMIN |
| 15 | ETHAN | LUKE | CALLUM | JAKE | ETHAN |
| 16 | GEORGE | CHARLIE | JAKE | ALFIE | LEWIS |
| 17 | ADAM | GEORGE | ETHAN | LUKE | MOHAMMED |
| 18 | ALFIE | CALLUM | GEORGE | MATTHEW | JAKE |
| 19 | CALLUM | ALEXANDER | LEWIS | ETHAN | DYLAN |
| 20 | ALEXANDER | MOHAMMED | ALEXANDER | LEWIS | JACOB |

|    | 2003 | 2004 | 2005 | 2006 | 2007 |
|----|------|------|------|------|------|
| 21 | RYAN | RYAN | JACOB | JACOB | LUKE |
| 22 | MOHAMMED | DYLAN | ALFIE | MOHAMMED | CALLUM |
| 23 | CAMERON | JACOB | MOHAMMED | DYLAN | ALEXANDER |
| 24 | CONNOR | ADAM | DYLAN | ALEXANDER | MATTHEW |
| 25 | CHARLIE | BEN | RYAN | RYAN | RYAN |
| 26 | BEN | JAKE | ADAM | ADAM | ADAM |
| 27 | JACOB | ALFIE | HARVEY | TYLER | TYLER |
| 28 | DYLAN | CONNOR | LIAM | HARVEY | LIAM |
| 29 | LIAM | CAMERON | MAX | MAX | HARVEY |
| 30 | NATHAN | LIAM | CONNOR | CAMERON | MAX |
| 31 | JAKE | NATHAN | TYLER | LIAM | HARRISON |
| 32 | JAMIE =* | HARVEY | BEN | JAMIE | JAYDEN |
| 33 | OWEN =* | JAMIE | JAMIE | LEO | CAMERON |
| 34 | MAX | OWEN | CAMERON | OWEN | HENRY |
| 35 | TYLER | TYLER | NATHAN | CONNOR | ARCHIE |
| 36 | HARVEY | MAX | OWEN | HARRISON | CONNOR |
| 37 | KIERAN | LOUIS | LEO | NATHAN | JAMIE |
| 38 | MICHAEL | KYLE | ARCHIE | BEN | MUHAMMAD |
| 39 | KYLE | MICHAEL | KYLE | HENRY | OSCAR |
| 40 | BRANDON | KIERAN | BRADLEY | ARCHIE | EDWARD |
| 41 | ALEX | AARON | HARRISON | EDWARD | LUCAS |
| 42 | LOUIS | BRADLEY | LOUIS | MICHAEL | ISAAC |
| 43 | AARON | EDWARD | MICHAEL | AARON | LEO |
| 44 | BRADLEY | BRANDON | HENRY | MUHAMMAD | OWEN |
| 45 | EDWARD =* | ALEX | EDWARD | KYLE | NATHAN |
| 46 | REECE =* | ARCHIE | AARON | NOAH | MICHAEL |
| 47 | HARRISON | HARRISON | BRANDON | OSCAR | FINLEY |
| 48 | CHARLES | HENRY | TOBY | LUCAS | BEN |
| 49 | DAVID | CHARLES | KIERAN | RHYS | AARON |
| 50 | ARCHIE | TOBY | CHARLES | BRADLEY | NOAH |

# Girls

| | 2003 | 2004 | 2005 | 2006 | 2007 |
|---|---|---|---|---|---|
| 1 | EMILY | EMILY | JESSICA | OLIVIA | GRACE |
| 2 | ELLIE | ELLIE | EMILY | GRACE | RUBY |
| 3 | CHLOE | JESSICA | SOPHIE | JESSICA | OLIVIA |
| 4 | JESSICA | SOPHIE | OLIVIA | RUBY | EMILY |
| 5 | SOPHIE | CHLOE | CHLOE | EMILY | JESSICA |
| 6 | MEGAN | LUCY | ELLIE | SOPHIE | SOPHIE |
| 7 | LUCY | OLIVIA | GRACE | CHLOE | CHLOE |
| 8 | OLIVIA | CHARLOTTE | LUCY | LUCY | LILY |
| 9 | CHARLOTTE | KATIE | CHARLOTTE | LILY | ELLA |
| 10 | HANNAH | MEGAN | KATIE | ELLIE | AMELIA |
| 11 | KATIE | GRACE | ELLA | ELLA | LUCY |
| 12 | ELLA | HANNAH | MEGAN | CHARLOTTE | CHARLOTTE |
| 13 | GRACE | AMY | HANNAH | KATIE | ELLIE |
| 14 | MIA | ELLA | AMELIA | MIA | MIA |
| 15 | AMY =* | MIA | RUBY | HANNAH | EVIE |
| 16 | HOLLY =* | LILY | LILY | AMELIA | HANNAH |
| 17 | LAUREN | ABIGAIL | AMY | MEGAN | MEGAN |
| 18 | EMMA | EMMA | MIA | AMY | KATIE |
| 19 | MOLLY | AMELIA | ABIGAIL | ISABELLA | ISABELLA |
| 20 | ABIGAIL | MOLLY | MILLIE | MILLIE | ISABELLE |
| 21 | CAITLIN | LAUREN | MOLLY | EVIE | MILLIE |
| 22 | AMELIA | MILLIE | EMMA | ABIGAIL | ABIGAIL |
| 23 | BETHANY | HOLLY | HOLLY | FREYA | AMY |
| 24 | LILY | LEAH | LEAH | MOLLY | DAISY |
| 25 | REBECCA | CAITLIN | ISABELLA | DAISY | FREYA |
| 26 | GEORGIA | REBECCA | LAUREN | HOLLY | EMMA |
| 27 | LEAH | GEORGIA | CAITLIN | EMMA | ERIN |
| 28 | MILLIE | BETHANY | DAISY | ERIN | POPPY |
| 29 | ELEANOR | ELEANOR | EVIE | ISABELLE | MOLLY |
| 30 | JASMINE | ISABELLE | ISABELLE | POPPY | HOLLY |
| 31 | DAISY | RUBY | FREYA | JASMINE | PHOEBE |
| 32 | ELIZABETH | DAISY | ERIN | LEAH | JASMINE |
| 33 | ALICE | FREYA | REBECCA | KEIRA | CAITLIN |

| | 2003 | 2004 | 2005 | 2006 | 2007 |
|---|---|---|---|---|---|
| 34 | COURTNEY | ISABELLA | GEORGIA | PHOEBE | IMOGEN |
| 35 | SHANNON | ELIZABETH | PHOEBE | CAITLIN | MADISON |
| 36 | ERIN | JASMINE | AMBER | REBECCA | ELIZABETH |
| 37 | ISABELLA | ERIN | MADISON | GEORGIA | SOPHIA |
| 38 | ABBIE | ALICE | KEIRA | LAUREN | KEIRA |
| 39 | ANNA | EVIE | POPPY | MADISON | SCARLETT |
| 40 | AMBER =* | AMBER | BETHANY | AMBER | LEAH |
| 41 | FREYA =* | PAIGE =* | JASMINE | ELIZABETH | AVA |
| 42 | ISABELLE | ABBIE =* | ELIZABETH | ELEANOR | GEORGIA |
| 43 | POPPY | MADISON | ELEANOR | BETHANY | ALICE |
| 44 | PAIGE | PHOEBE | ALICE | ISABEL | SUMMER |
| 45 | PHOEBE | POPPY | PAIGE | PAIGE | ISABEL |
| 46 | SARAH | AIMEE =* | ISABEL | SCARLETT | REBECCA |
| 47 | ISABEL | COURTNEY=* | SCARLETT | ALICE | LAUREN |
| 48 | RACHEL | NIAMH | LIBBY | IMOGEN | AMBER |
| 49 | AIMEE | ANNA | AIMEE | SOPHIA | ELEANOR |
| 50 | RUBY | ISABEL | NIAMH | ANNA | BETHANY |

# Other trends

## Unique names

A noticeable trend in recent years is to give children very unusual names. In a bid to escape the perils of names that swarm in and out of fashion, or choosing names which are shared by three other classmates, more and more parents are striving to be more individual and creative.

Using words that previously haven't been names is one option parents are choosing and, ironically enough, the name Unique has become popular for the first time. Using other modern-day words such as Happy, Ocean and Autumn is also a new fad. Another way to give your child a more individualized name is to adapt the spelling. Traditional names such as Lily have become Lillie; Jackson becomes Jaxxon. Other parents have resorted to unusual ethnic names, place names (Brooklyn) or surnames as first names.

The ultimate way, of course, to minimize the chance that anyone on the planet will share your baby's name is simply to make it up.

### The pros

A unique name will remain memorable and a symbol of your child's individuality. After a long day of job interviews, any would-be employer will be more likely to remember Amerique than Amy and people will be more intrigued when introduced to Serendipity at a dinner party than Sarah.

### The cons

You will have to be careful when choosing your unique name that you don't fall into the trap of using naming techniques which in themselves are becoming faddish and will therefore produce names that aren't as unique as you hope – for example, altering spellings: using k instead of c (Vikki); x instead of k (Jaxon); or using words for moods or states of mind (Serendipity or Bliss). If you love the name, it doesn't really matter of course, but be aware that it might make the name seem dated in a few years' time.

## Celtic names

Another recent trend in baby names has been a huge rise in the popularity of Scottish, Welsh, Irish and Cornish names. Kyle, Kieran, Callum and Connor are now in the 100 most popular boys' names, with Erin, Caitlin and Niamh in the girls' top 100. For some this may be a reference back to their family roots, for others they may have been inspired by Celtic celebrities such as Callum Best and Ioan Gruffudd. Others just find a name they love. Many Celtic names such as Alan and Gareth have become so well-used that people rarely consider their origin.

### The pros

Many Celtic names are beautiful, poetic names which are evocative of the rugged landscapes in which the names were inspired. It can be a wonderful way to pay tribute to your ancestral connections, and owing to the fact that spellings and pronunciation of Celtic and Gaelic inspired names is not the norm for most people, the names are often naturally memorable and unusual.

### The cons

The spellings and pronunciations can equally be the bane of your life and eventually your child's as you carefully annunciate and spell your way through countless phone calls and new introductions. People will often get the name wrong, and no matter how used to this you are, it can be irritating and sometimes hurtful when people you feel know you well make the mistake. And if your Celtic connections are very tenuous, you may find yourself viewed by real Celts in years to come with some cynicism.

## Predicting future trends

The best way to predict future trends is often to look to the past. It's clear from recent decades that most names inspired by celebrities tend to date very quickly. It's also clear that, in most cases, names which spend a long time heading the league tables begin to lose favour. Joshua is a case in point: after five years in the top three boys' names, it is now starting to fall from grace.

## Most popular baby names: 1904 to 1999

[Source: *Office of National Statistics*]

| Boys | 1904 | 1934 | 1964 | 1994 | 1999 |
|---|---|---|---|---|---|
| 1 | WILLIAM | JOHN | DAVID | THOMAS | JACK |
| 2 | JOHN | PETER | PAUL | JAMES | THOMAS |
| 3 | GEORGE | WILLIAM | ANDREW | JACK | JAMES |
| 4 | THOMAS | BRIAN | MARK | DANIEL | DANIEL |
| 5 | ARTHUR | DAVID | JOHN | MATTHEW | JOSHUA |

| Girls | 1904 | 1934 | 1964 | 1994 | 1999 |
|---|---|---|---|---|---|
| 1 | MARY | MARGARET | SUSAN | REBECCA | CHLOE |
| 2 | FLORENCE | JEAN | JULIE | LAUREN | EMILY |
| 3 | DORIS | MARY | KAREN | JESSICA | MEGAN |
| 4 | EDITH | JOAN | JACQUELINE/ CHARLOTTE | CHARLOTTE | OLIVIA |
| 5 | DOROTHY | PATRICIA | DEBORAH | HANNAH | SOPHIE |

# The desire to be unique

Other trends which people seem to have used in an attempt to be unique fall out of favour quickly, simply because the parents who favour this creative and individual style of name will want to avoid those fads entirely. Unusual spellings of names such as Hayden, for Jayden, which appear in the popularity lists, are likely to disappear within a year or two of appearing. Likewise, names like Unique, which become the polar opposite of their intended meaning are likely to shoot down the rankings. And boys' names which are used for girls, such as Ashley, in an attempt for individuality, are unlikely to remain a long-lasting favourite.

Equally, it pays to look at the current major influences on modern-day society. The fact that many of us are now identified by PIN numbers and barcodes is likely to have played a part in the current popularity of very unique and individual names. This trend towards de-personalization shows no sign of changing, in an age where we're increasingly computer-coded or asked to quote a reference number instead of our name, so it's likely the trend for individual and unique names will continue to thrive.

If you're looking for new trends that are likely to arrive soon, it may be worth noting the cyclical nature of name fashions. Following popularity tables, waves of names seem to make a comeback every three generations. The Marthas and Tillys born in the early twentieth century are now seeing their great grandchildren christened in their honour and, if the cycle holds true, names which were popular in the 1930s and 1940s, such as Mary, Joan and Brian, may be next to make a comeback.

Another way to get ahead of your time is to anticipate the backlash. While it might be hippy chic and bohemian to name your child Leaf or Summer in a time when we're all too aware of how precious the natural world is, it's possible that environmentally-friendly names may give way to the likes of Diesel, Jet and Carbon becoming the next big thing.

Of course, if you're reading this 20 years from now, and Unique has been the most popular girls' name for the last 15 years, it will be proof of one perennial truth – there are no cast iron guarantees when it comes to predicting the future.

## How to choose a timeless name

If you want to avoid the ebb and flow of baby-name trends altogether and choose a name that simply won't date, the simplest option is to look to names which have proved their longevity and which have remained popular for centuries. Biblical names such as Rachel, Sarah and Rebecca have been loved for centuries by parents of girls; Thomas, Peter and David remain popular for boys despite the fads and fashions of the passing years. Other sources to look to are popular names from mythology and legend, such as Jason, Diana and Helen.

If you want the name to truly remain timeless, don't use a spelling which is more fashionable at the moment – fashions, by definition, date. Instead use the spellings which have remained well used for a long time.

Some ancient and well-loved names such as Jennifer (which originally comes from Guinevere, in the legend of King Arthur) can go through phases of overkill – Jennifer remained one of the most popular girls names in the US for 15 years. But although they may go through some years of unpopularity as a result, it's unlikely they'll ever fall out of favour entirely.

# 04

## boys' names
## a to z

**In this chapter you will learn:**
- the origin of your favourite names
- the meaning of your favourite names
- alternative spellings and names that sound similar.

| Name | Alternate spellings | Origin | Meaning |
|------|--------------------|--------|---------|

## A

| Name | Alternate spellings | Origin | Meaning |
|------|--------------------|--------|---------|
| Aaron | | Hebrew | Exalted one |
| Abbas | Ab, Abba | Arabic | Harsh |
| Abbondanzio | | Italian | Plentiful |
| Abbondio | | Italian | Plentiful |
| Abbott | Abbitt, Abott | Hebrew | Father |
| Abdalla | | African | Servant of God |
| Abdel | Abdiel | Arabic | Servant |
| Abdul | Ab, Abul | African | Servant of the Lord |
| Abdullah | Abdallah, | Arabic | The servant of Allah |
| Abe | Abey | Hebrew | Short for Abraham, father of many |
| Abedi | | African | Worshipper |
| Abejundio | | Spanish | Like a bee |
| Abel | Abe | Hebrew | Breath, vapour. Murdered by his brother, Cain, in the Bible |
| Abelard | Abe, Abellard | German | Firm |
| Abelardo | | Italian | Like a bee |
| Abele | | Italian | White poplar |
| Aberdeen | | Place name | Scottish city |
| Aberforth | | Scottish | Mouth of the River Forth |
| Abiola | | African | Born in honour |
| Abir | | Arabic | The fragrant one |
| Abner | Abnor | Hebrew | Father of light |
| Abraham | Abe | Hebrew | Father of a multitude |
| Abram | Abrahm, Abe | Hebrew | Father of a multitude |
| Abramo | | Italian | Father of a multitude |

| Name | Alternate spellings | Origin | Meaning |
|------|---------------------|--------|---------|
| Ace | | American | Nickname for someone who's the best |
| Achilles | | Greek | Legendary warrior in Greek mythology |
| Acorn | | English | The seed of an oak tree |
| Adalfredo | | Italian | He who protects his descendants |
| Adalgiso | | Italian | Precious promise |
| Adalrico | | Italian | Noble ruler |
| Adam | Addam | Hebrew | Red earth |
| Addison | | Hebrew | Son of Adam |
| Adelbert | | German | Noble and bright |
| Adil | | Arabic | Just, fair |
| Adnan | | Arabic | The settler |
| Adolf | Adolph | German | Noble wolf |
| Adoni | | Australian | Sunset |
| Adonis | | Greek | Beautiful man. Lover of Venus |
| Adrian | Ade, Adrien | Latin | Dark, rich, from Hadria |
| Adriano | | Italian | Dark, rich, from Hadria |
| Adriel | Adrial, Adryal | Hebrew | God's follower |
| Afanasi | | Russian | Immortal |
| Afram | | African | A river in Ghana |
| Agatino | | Italian | Good |
| Agustin | | Spanish | Great, magnificent |
| Ahmed | | Arabic | Most highly praised |
| Ahron | | Hebrew | Exalted one |
| Aidan | Adan | Irish | Fiery one |
| Aimé | | French | Loved |
| Ainsley | | Anglo-Saxon | My own meadow |

| Name | Alternate spellings | Origin | Meaning |
|------|--------------------|--------|---------|
| Ajax | | Greek | Mythical Greek hero |
| Akama | | Australian | A whale |
| Akbar | | Arabic | Great |
| Ake | | Scandinavian | Ancestor |
| Akeem | | Arabic | Ruler |
| Akil | | Arabic | Intelligent |
| Akim | | Russian | Joachim |
| Akram | | Arabic | Generous, noble |
| Al | | | Short for several names, Alan, Alfred, etc. |
| Aladdin | | Arabic | A servant of Allah |
| Alain | | French | Handsome |
| Alan | | Scottish, Irish | Handsome |
| Alarico | | Italian, Spanish | Rules all |
| Alasdair | Alastair | Scottish | Defender of mankind |
| Alban | | Latin | White |
| Alberico | | Italian | Noble and bright |
| Albert | | Anglo-Saxon | Noble and bright |
| Alberto | | Italian | Noble and bright |
| Albion | | Latin | White, poetic name for Britain |
| Albus | | Latin | White |
| Alden | | Anglo-Saxon | Old friend |
| Aldo | | Italian | Old |
| Aldon | | Anglo-Saxon | Old friend |
| Aldous | | German | Old |
| Aldwin | | Anglo-Saxon | Old friend |
| Alec | | French | Defender of mankind |
| Alejandro | | Spanish | Defender of mankind |

| Name | Alternate spellings | Origin | Meaning |
|---|---|---|---|
| Alek | | Russian | Defender of mankind |
| Aleksander | | Russian | Defender of mankind |
| Aleksei | | Russian | Defender of mankind |
| Aleppo | | Place name | City in Syria |
| Aleron | | French | Knight |
| Alessio | | Italian | Defender of mankind |
| Alex | | Greek | Defender of mankind |
| Alexander | | Greek | Defender of mankind |
| Alexandre | | French | Defender of mankind |
| Alexei | | Russian | Defender of mankind |
| Alexis | | Greek | Defender of mankind |
| Alfie | | Anglo-Saxon | Elf/wise counsellor. From Alfred |
| Alfonso | | Italian, Spanish | Ready for battle |
| Alfred | | Anglo-Saxon | Elf/wise counsellor |
| Alfredo | | Italian | Wise counsellor |
| Algar | | Anglo-Saxon | Elf spear |
| Alger | | Anglo-Saxon | Elf spear |
| Ali | | Arabic | Exalted |
| Alim | | Arabic | Wise |
| Alistair | | Scottish | Defender of mankind |
| Alister | | Irish | Defender of mankind |
| Allambee | | Australian | A quiet resting place |
| Allan | Allyn, Alan, Alun, Allen | Irish | Handsome |

| Name | Alternate spellings | Origin | Meaning |
|------|---------------------|--------|---------|
| Alonso | | Spanish | Noble and ready |
| Alun | Allyn, Alan, Allen | Welsh | Handsome |
| Alvaro | | Italian, Spanish | Speaker of truth |
| Alvin | | Anglo-Saxon | Elf friend |
| Alwyn | | Anglo-Saxon | Elf friend |
| Amadeus | | Latin | Loves God. Name of Wolfgang Amadeus Mozart, famous composer |
| Amador | | Spanish | Lover |
| Amal | | Arabic | Hope |
| Amalio | | Italian | Lively, determined |
| Amaranto | | Italian | Long lived |
| Amaroo | | Australian | A beautiful place |
| Amato | | Spanish | Beloved |
| Amaury | | French | Hard-working, powerful |
| Ambar | | Sanskrit | Of the sky |
| Ambrose | | Greek | Immortal |
| America | | Place name | America is named from Italian explorer Amerigo Vespucci |
| Amerigo | | Italian | Home ruler |
| Amin | | Arabic | Honest and trustworthy |
| Amir | | Arabic | Prince |
| Amis | | French | Variant of Ames, friend |
| Amistad | | Spanish | Friendship |
| Amory | | German | Ruler of the home |

| Name | Alternate spellings | Origin | Meaning |
|------|---------------------|--------|---------|
| Amos | | Hebrew | Borne by God |
| Amrit | | Sanskrit | The immortal one |
| Amund | | Scandinavian | Feared protector |
| Anand | | Sanskrit | Joyful |
| Anatole | | Greek | From the East |
| Ancel | | French | Servant |
| Anders | | Scandinavian | Manly |
| André | | French | Manly |
| Andrei | | Russian | Manly |
| Andrew | Andy, Drew | Greek | Manly |
| Andy | | Greek | Manly |
| Angelo | | Italian | Angel |
| Anghus | Angus | Scottish | Exceptionally strong |
| Anil | | Sanskrit | Of the wind |
| Anisim | | Russian | Beneficial, profitable |
| Ansari | | Arabic | A helper |
| Anselm | | German | God's helmet |
| Anthony | Tony | Latin | Worthy of praise |
| Antoine | | French | Praiseworthy |
| Anton | | French | Praiseworthy |
| Antonio | | Italian, Spanish | Worthy of praise |
| Anwar | | Arabic | The bright one |
| Anwell | | Welsh | Beloved |
| Anwyl | | Welsh | Beloved |
| Aonghus | | Celtic | Exceptionally strong |
| Apollo | | Greek | God of poetry, music and healing |
| Aragorn | | Literary | *Lord of the Rings* by J. R. R. Tolkien |
| Araluen | | Australian | The place of water lilies |
| Aram | | Hebrew | Father of a multitude |

| Name | Alternate spellings | Origin | Meaning |
|------|---------------------|--------|---------|
| Aramis | | Literary | *The Three Musketeers* by Alexandre Dumas |
| Arcadio | | Greek | Man from Arcadia, paradise |
| Archibald | Archie, Baldie | German | Genuine, brave |
| Archie | | Scottish | Genuine, brave |
| Archimedes | | Greek | To think about first |
| Arcturus | | Greek | Bear driver. The star which follows the Great Bear constellation |
| Ardent | | English | Keen |
| Argus | | Greek | In mythology, a giant with 100 eyes |
| Ari | Are | Scandinavian | Eagle |
| Ariel | | Hebrew | Lion of God |
| Aries | | Greek | The ram. A star sign and constellation |
| Ariki | | Pacific Islands | Chief |
| Arion | Ari Arie | Greek | Enchanted man |
| Ariosto | | Italian | Quick to fight |
| Aristo | | Greek | Best |
| Arizona | | Place name | US state |
| Arjun | | Sanskrit | The white one |
| Arlin | Arlyn | Welsh | Vow |
| Armand | Armande | French | From the army |
| Armando | | Italian, Spanish | Of the army |
| Armani | | French | Warrior. Surname of fashion designer, Giorgio Armani |
| Armstrong | | Anglo-Saxon | Strong-armed |

| Name | Alternate spellings | Origin | Meaning |
|------|---------------------|--------|---------|
| Arnaud | | French | Eagle power |
| Arnold | Arnie | German | Eagle, ruler |
| Aron | | Hebrew | Exalted one |
| Arran | | Place name | From the Isle of Arran |
| Artemas | Artie | Greek | From Artemis Goddess of the moon and hunting |
| Arthur | Artur | Welsh, Cornish | Bear |
| Artie | | Welsh, Cornish | Bear |
| Arun | | Sanskrit | The dawn |
| Arvid | | Scandinavian | Eagle, tree |
| Ash | | Anglo-Saxon | A tree |
| Ashley | Ash | Anglo-Saxon | From the meadow of ash trees |
| Ashok | | Sanskrit | Without sadness |
| Ashraf | | Arabic | Honourable |
| Asim | | Arabic | The protector |
| Asmund | | Scandinavian | Divine protection |
| Aston | | Anglo-Saxon | Eastern town |
| Aswad | | Arabic | Black |
| Athan | | Greek | Immortal |
| Atiu | | Pacific Islands | Firstborn |
| Aubrey | Aubry, Aubree | Anglo-Saxon | Elfin king |
| Auden | | Anglo-Saxon | Old friend |
| Audey | | American | Famous US solider |
| Auguste | | French | Noble, magnificent |
| Augustin | | French | Noble, magnificent |
| Aurelius | | Latin | The golden one |
| Austell | | Place name | Cornish town, St Austell |

| Name | Alternate spellings | Origin | Meaning |
|------|---------------------|--------|---------|
| Austin | Austen Ostin, Ostyn | Latin | From Augustine, great, magnificent |
| Avalon | | Celtic | An island paradise in Celtic mythology |
| Avery | | Anglo-Saxon | Elfin king |
| Avon | | Place name | From several English rivers |
| Axel | | Scandinavian | Father of peace |
| Azim | | Arabic | Grand |
| Aziz | | Arabic | The powerful one |
| Azriel | | Hebrew | God helps |

| Name | Alternate spellings | Origin | Meaning |
|------|---------------------|--------|---------|
| **B** | | | |
| Baakir | | African | Eldest |
| Babu | | African | Grandfather |
| Babylon | | Place name | Ancient city in the Middle East |
| Badrani | | African | Full Moon |
| Bailey | | French | Bailiff |
| Bairrie | | Irish | Fair-haired or marksman |
| Balthasar | Balthazar | Greek | The Lord protects the king. One of the three wise men |
| Balun | | Australian | A river |
| Banjora | | Australian | A koala |
| Barclay | | Anglo-Saxon | From the birch tree meadow |
| Bardan | Barden | Welsh | Singer, poet |
| Bardo | | Australian | Water |
| Barega | | Australian | The wind |
| Barlow | | American | Lives on a bare hill |
| Barnabas | Barney, Barny | Greek | Son of consolation |
| Barnaby | Barney, Barny | Greek | Son of consolation |
| Barney | Barnie | Anglo-Saxon | Son of comfort |
| Baron | | Anglo-Saxon | Young warrior |
| Barrington | | Place name | Name of English villages |
| Barry | Barrie | Irish | Fair head, marksman |
| Bartemius | Bartie | Anglo-Saxon | Hill, furrow |
| Bartholomew | Bart, Bartie | Anglo-Saxon | Ploughman |
| Barton | | Anglo-Saxon | From the barley town |
| Barwon | | Australian | Wide river |

| Name | Alternate spellings | Origin | Meaning |
|------|---------------------|--------|---------|
| Bashir | | Arabic | A good omen |
| Basil | | Greek | Like a king |
| Basim | | Arabic | The smiling one |
| Basso | | Italian | Low |
| Baxter | | Anglo-Saxon | Baker |
| Beau | | French | Handsome |
| Beaumont | | French | From the beautiful mountain |
| Beethoven | | Anglo-Saxon | Famous composer |
| Bello | | African | Helper |
| Ben | | Latin | Son |
| Benedict | | Latin | Blessed |
| Benesek | | Cornish | Blessed |
| Benito | | Italian | Blessed |
| Benjamin | Ben | Latin | Born of the right hand |
| Bennet | | Latin | Blessed |
| Bennett | | Latin | Blessed |
| Benno | | Italian | Blessed |
| Benoît | | French | Blessed |
| Benson | Ben | Latin | Blessed |
| Benton | | Anglo-Saxon | Town in the bent grass |
| Bernard | | Anglo-Saxon | Brave as a bear |
| Bernardo | | Italian | Brave as a bear |
| Bernhard | Bernie | German | Strong as a bear |
| Berthold | Bert | German | Bright, splendid |
| Bertoldo | | Italian | Illustrious leader |
| Bertram | | Anglo-Saxon | Bright raven |
| Bertrand | | French | Bright raven |
| Bevan | Bevin, Bevyn | Welsh | Young warrior |
| Bharat | | Sanskrit | The Hindu God of fire |
| Bhima | | Sanskrit | The mighty one |
| Biagio | | Italian | One who stammers |

| Name | Alternate spellings | Origin | Meaning |
|------|---------------------|--------|---------|
| Bilal | | Arabic | Follower of Mohammed |
| Bill | | Anglo-Saxon | Strong protector |
| Billy | Billie | Anglo-Saxon | Strong protector |
| Bjorn | | Scandinavian | Bear |
| Blaine | Blane, Blayne | Irish | Slender |
| Blair | Blare, Blaire | Irish | Lives on the plain |
| Blaise | Blaze, Blaisey, Blazey | Latin | One who stammers |
| Blake | | Anglo-Saxon | Black |
| Blanket | | Celebrity child | (Michael Jackson) |
| Blayney | Blaney, Blainey | Irish | Slender |
| Blue | | English | Primary colour |
| Bobby | Bob | Anglo-Saxon | Short for Robert, bright fame |
| Boden | | Welsh | Blonde |
| Bogdan | | Russian | Gift from God |
| Bond | | Anglo-Saxon | Peasant farmer |
| Bones | | American | Means 'bones', as in the English |
| Bonifacio | | Italian | Good destiny |
| Booker | | American | Bookmaker |
| Boone | | American | Wild-west frontier hero |
| Boris | | Russian | Famous warrior |
| Bosley | | Anglo-Saxon | From the grove |
| Boston | | Place name | American city |
| Bowden | | Welsh | Blonde |
| Bowen | Bowyn | Welsh | Son of Owen |
| Bowie | | Welsh | Yellow haired |
| Boyd | | Scottish | Fair haired |
| Brad | | American | Clearing in the wood |
| Bradan | | Welsh | Raven |

| Name | Alternate spellings | Origin | Meaning |
|------|---------------------|--------|---------|
| Bradford | | Anglo-Saxon | Broad ford |
| Bradley | | American | Broad forest clearing |
| Bram | | Welsh | Raven |
| Bramwell | | Anglo-Saxon | Broom well |
| Bran | Brann | Welsh | Raven |
| Brando | | American | Talented |
| Brandon | | Anglo-Saxon | Gorse hill |
| Branson | | Anglo-Saxon | Son of Brandon |
| Brant | | American | From welsh Brent, hilltop |
| Brave | | English | Courageous |
| Brecon | | Place name | From Brecon Beacons in Wales |
| Brendan | | Irish | Raven |
| Brennan | | Welsh | Little raven |
| Brent | | Welsh | Hilltop |
| Bret | Brett | Welsh | From Brittany |
| Brian | | Irish, Scottish | High, noble |
| Brighton | | Place name | Seaside town on south coast of England |
| Brock | | Anglo-Saxon | Badger |
| Broder | Brody | Scandinavian | Brother |
| Broderick | | Irish | Son of a famous ruler |
| Brody | | Irish | A ditch |
| Bron | | Anglo-Saxon | Brown or dark |
| Bronson | | Anglo-Saxon | Son of the dark man |
| Bronze | | Anglo-Saxon | Precious metal |
| Brook | | Anglo-Saxon | A small stream |
| Brooklyn | | Place name | Area in New York. Also celebrity child (David and Victoria Beckham) |

| Name | Alternate spellings | Origin | Meaning |
|------|---------------------|--------|---------|
| Brown | | Anglo-Saxon | Colour |
| Bruno | | German,Italian | Brown |
| Bryan | | Irish, Scottish | High, noble |
| Bryce | | Welsh | Strength |
| Bryn | | Welsh | Hill |
| Bubba | | American | Slang for baby |
| Buck | | American | Slang for a dollar |
| Bud | | Anglo-Saxon | Brother |
| Buddy | | Anglo-Saxon | Brother |
| Butch | | American | Macho |
| Byron | | Anglo-Saxon | At the cowshed |

| Name | Alternate spellings | Origin | Meaning |
|------|---------------------|--------|---------|
| **C** | | | |
| Cadan | | Welsh | Warrior |
| Cade | | Literary | *Gone with the Wind* by Margaret Mitchell |
| Cador | | Cornish | Warrior |
| Cadwur | | Welsh | Warrior |
| Caelum | | Latin | Constellation names after a sculptor's chisel |
| Cai | | Welsh | Joy |
| Cain | | Hebrew | Gatherer. Son of Adam and Eve who killed his brother in the bible |
| Caio | | Welsh | Joy |
| Cairo | | Place name | Capital of Egypt |
| Cal | | Scottish, Irish | Dove |
| Cale | | Hebrew | Short form of 'Caleb' |
| Caleb | | Hebrew | Faithful dog |
| Calhoun | | American | From the narrow forest |
| Callum | Calum | Scottish, Irish | Dove |
| Calm | | English | Tranquil |
| Calvin | | Latin | Little bald one |
| Cam | | Scottish | Crooked mouth |
| Cameron | | Scottish | Crooked nose |
| Camillo | | Italian | Ceremonial attendant/ freedom |
| Camilo | | French | Ceremonial attendant/ freedom |
| Campbell | | Scottish | Crooked mouth |

| Name | Alternate spellings | Origin | Meaning |
|------|---------------------|--------|---------|
| Cane | | Hebrew | Variant of Cain, son of Adam and Eve who killed his brother in the Bible |
| Caradoc | | Cornish, Welsh | Lovable |
| Caradwg | | Welsh | Lovable |
| Carbry | | Irish | Charioteer |
| Carisio | | Italian | Beauty, grace |
| Carl | Karl | German | Free man |
| Carlo | | Italian | Manly |
| Carlos | | Spanish | Manly |
| Carlyle | | Place name | Town in the north of England |
| Carmel | | Hebrew | Garden, orchard |
| Carrington | | Anglo-Saxon | Place name and surname |
| Carson | | American | Son who lives in a swamp |
| Cary | | Welsh | Descendant of the dark one |
| Casey | | Irish | Brave |
| Cash | | English | Money |
| Caspar | Kaspar | Scandinavian | From the gem Jasper |
| Caspian | | Literary | *Prince Caspian* by C. S. Lewis |
| Cassidy | | Irish | Clever |
| Cassio | | Italian | Empty, hollow |
| Cassius | | Latin | Empty, hollow |
| Castel | | Spanish | Castle |
| Castor | | Greek | One of the twin stars of the constellation Gemini |
| Caton | | Spanish | Wise |

| Name | Alternate spellings | Origin | Meaning |
|------|---------------------|--------|---------|
| Cecil | | Latin | The blind one |
| Cedric | Cederic | Literary | *Ivanhoe* by Sir Walter Scott |
| Celio | | Italian, Spanish | Heavenly |
| Cemal | | Arabic | Perfect |
| Cesare | | Italian | Hairy |
| Chacha | | African | Strong |
| Chad | | Anglo-Saxon | Warrior |
| Chale | | Spanish | Boy |
| Chance | | American | Gambler or lucky person |
| Chandan | | Sanskrit | Of the Sandalwood tree |
| Chandler | | Anglo-Saxon | Candlemaker |
| Chandra | | Sanskrit | Bright moon |
| Charles | Charlie, Chaz | French | Free man |
| Charlie | Chaz | French | Free man |
| Chase | | French | Hunter |
| Chaz | | American | From Charles, free man |
| Chester | | Latin | Roman site or camp |
| Chevalier | | French | Knight |
| Chibale | | African | Kinship |
| Chimalsi | | African | Proud |
| Chopin | | Anglo-Saxon | Famous composer |
| Christhard | | German | Brave Christian |
| Christian | | Latin | Follower of Christ |
| Christophe | | French | Bearer of Christ |
| Christopher | | Greek | Bearer of Christ. Patron saint of travellers |
| Chuck | | American | From Charles, free man |
| Churchill | | English | From Winston Churchill |
| Ciaran | | Welsh | Little dark one |
| Cicero | | Latin | A chickpea or bean |

| Name | Alternate spellings | Origin | Meaning |
|------|---------------------|--------|---------|
| Cid | | Spanish | Lord |
| Cipriano | | Italian | From Cyprus |
| Cirrus | | Anglo-Saxon | A form of cloud |
| Clancy | | Irish | Lively |
| Clarence | | Latin | Clear, luminous |
| Clark | Clerk, Clarke | Latin | Clerk |
| Claude | Claud | Latin | The lame one |
| Claudio | | Italian, Spanish | Lame one |
| Claus | Klaus | German | People's victory |
| Clay | | American | From Clayton |
| Clayton | | American | Town on clay land |
| Clement | | Latin | Gentle, merciful |
| Cliff | | Anglo-Saxon | Ford by the cliff |
| Clifford | | Anglo-Saxon | Ford by the cliff |
| Clint | | Anglo-Saxon | Town by the cliff |
| Clinton | | Anglo-Saxon | Town by the cliff |
| Clive | | Anglo-Saxon | Cliff by the river |
| Cloud | | Anglo-Saxon | Water vapour in the sky |
| Clyde | | Scottish | Warm |
| Cobain | | American | Surname used as a first name. Surname of famous lead singer of Nirvana, Kurt Cobain |
| Cobalt | | English | Silver grey metal |
| Cobar | | Australian | Burnt earth |
| Cody | Codie | Irish | Cushion |
| Cohen | Kohen | Hebrew | From Kohen, meaning priest |
| Colbert | | German | Famous protector |
| Colby | | Anglo-Saxon | Dark |
| Coleman | | Scottish, Irish | Dove |
| Colin | | Irish | Young cub |

| Name | Alternate spellings | Origin | Meaning |
|------|---------------------|--------|---------|
| Colm | | Irish | Dove |
| Conall | | Scottish | Strong wolf |
| Conan | | Irish | Wolf, hound. Legendary Irish hero |
| Concordio | | Italian | Agreeable |
| Conn | | Irish | Chief, leader |
| Conor | Connor | Irish | Lover of hounds |
| Conrad | | German | Brave advisor |
| Cooper | | Anglo-Saxon | Barrel maker |
| Coorain | | Australian | The wind |
| Corey | Cory | Irish | Lives near a hollow |
| Cormac | | Irish | Raven's son |
| Cornelio | | Italian, Spanish | From Cornelius |
| Cornelius | | Latin | Roman solider who became a Christian |
| Cortes | | Spanish | Victorious |
| Cosimo | | Italian | Order, decency |
| Cosmo | | Greek | Harmony |
| Costanzo | | Italian | Steadfast |
| Courtney | | Anglo-Saxon | Courtier |
| Craig | | Scottish | Rock |
| Creighton | | Place name | Near the creek |
| Crispin | | Latin | Curly haired |
| Cristiano | | Italian | Follower of Christ |
| Cristo | | Spanish | Follower of Christ |
| Cruze | Cruz | Spanish | Cross |
| Cupid | | Latin | Son of Venus, a god of love |
| Curtis | | Anglo-Saxon | Courteous |
| Cuthbert | | Anglo-Saxon | Famous |
| Cyclone | | Anglo-Saxon | Powerful and destructive weather system |
| Cyril | | Greek | Lordly |

| Name | Alternate spellings | Origin | Meaning |
|------|--------------------|--------|---------|
| **D** | | | |
| Dadrian | | American | From Adrian (from Hadria, place in Italy) |
| Daffyd | | Welsh | Beloved |
| Dahl | | Scandinavian | Norwegian surname, name of Roald Dahl, famous children's author |
| Dai | | Welsh | To shine |
| Dakota | | American | US place name, American Indian Tribe |
| Daktari | | African | Healer |
| Daku | | Australian | Sand |
| Daley | | Irish | Gathering |
| Dalziel | | Scottish | Small field |
| Damien | Damian, Damon | Greek | True friend |
| Dan | | Hebrew | God is my judge |
| Daniel | | Hebrew | God is my judge |
| Danil | | Russian | God is my judge |
| Danny | | Hebrew | God is my judge |
| Dante | | Italian | Enduring |
| Darby | | Place name | From Derby, deer settlement |
| Darcy | | Irish | Dark |
| Darel | | Australian | Blue sky |
| Darell | | French | Beloved |
| Daric | | Irish | Ruler of the people |
| Darien | | Greek | Wealthy |
| Darien | | Spanish | Uncertain |
| Dario | | Italian | He who possesses good things |

| Name | Alternate spellings | Origin | Meaning |
|---|---|---|---|
| Darius | | Greek | He who possesses good things |
| Darragh | | Irish, Scottish | Dark oak |
| Darren | | Anglo-Saxon | Uncertain |
| Darrick | | Irish | Ruler of the people |
| Darrick | | American | From Derrick (famous ruler) |
| Darryl | | French | From Ariele, in France |
| Dartagnan | | French | Leader |
| Darwin | | English | Australian city and name of famous scientist Charles Darwin |
| Dary | | Irish | Wealthy |
| Dave | | Hebrew | Beloved |
| David | | Hebrew | Beloved |
| Davin | | Welsh | Beloved |
| Davon | | American | From Devon, English county |
| Deacon | | Greek | Messenger |
| Dean | | Latin | A soldier |
| Decca | | Greek | Ten |
| Declan | | Irish | Man of prayer |
| Dedalus | | Greek | In mythology builder of the Minotaurs labyrinth and Icarus' father |
| Deepak | | Sanskrit | Like a lamp or light |
| Delaney | | Irish | Son of the challenger |
| Dell | | Anglo-Saxon | Hollow or valley |
| Demetrio | | Italian | From Demeter, Greek goddess of agriculture |

| Name | Alternate spellings | Origin | Meaning |
|------|---------------------|--------|---------|
| Demetrius | | Spanish | From Demeter, Greek goddess of agriculture |
| Dempsey | | Irish | Proud |
| Denby | | Anglo-Saxon | From the Danish settlement |
| Dennis | | Greek | Wild. Lover of wine |
| Denton | | Anglo-Saxon | Settlement in the valley |
| Denver | | Place name | US city |
| Denzel | | Cornish | Cornish surname and place name |
| Deo | | Greek | God-like |
| Derain | | Australian | Of the mountains |
| Dermot | | Irish | Free of envy |
| Desidirio | | Italian, Spanish | Desire |
| Desmond | | Irish | Man from south Munster |
| Dev | | Sanskrit | Godlike |
| Devante | | Spanish | From a Spanish aristocratic surname |
| Devdan | | Sanskrit | The gift of the gods |
| Devin | | Irish | Poet |
| Devlyn | | Irish | Brave |
| Devon | | Place name | English county |
| Dewey | | American | Welsh surname and place name, pet form of David, which means beloved |
| Dexter | | Latin | Right handed, dexterous |
| Dheran | | Australian | A gully |
| Diallo | | African | Bold |

| Name | Alternate spellings | Origin | Meaning |
|------|---------------------|--------|---------|
| Diarmaid | | Irish | Free of envy |
| Didier | | French | Desired |
| Diego | | Italian, Spanish | Teacher |
| Dieter | | German | People's army |
| Diezel Ky | | Celebrity child | (Toni Braxton and Keri Lewis) |
| Digby | | Anglo-Saxon | Ditch town |
| Diggory | | French | Lost |
| Dillan | | Welsh | Celtic god associated with the sea |
| Dillon | | Welsh | Celtic god associated with the sea |
| Dima | | Russian | From Demeter, Greek goddess of agriculture |
| Dimitri | | Russian | From Demeter, Greek goddess of agriculture |
| Dinesh | | Sanskrit | The lord of the day |
| Dirk | | American | From Derek |
| Dmitri | | Russian | From Demeter, Greek goddess of agriculture |
| Dobby | | Literary | 'House elf' in the *Harry Potter* novels |
| Dolph | | German | Short for Adolph, noble wolf |
| Domenico | | Italian | Belonging to God |
| Domhnall | | Scottish | World ruler |
| Dominic | | Latin | Belonging to God |
| Dominique | | French | Belonging to God |

| Name | Alternate spellings | Origin | Meaning |
|------|---------------------|--------|---------|
| Donal | | Scottish | World ruler |
| Donald | Don | Scottish | World ruler |
| Donatien | | French | Gift |
| Donovan | | Irish | Dark-haired chief |
| Dorado | | Spanish | Swordfish, a constellation |
| Dorak | | Australian | Lively |
| Dorian | | Literary | *The Picture of Dorian Gray* by Oscar Wilde |
| Dougal | | Scottish | Dark stranger |
| Douglas | Doug | Scottish | Dark river |
| Doyle | | Irish | Dark stranger |
| Draco | | Latin | Dragon. A constellation |
| Drake | | Irish | Dark stranger |
| Drew | | Greek | Manly |
| Dudley | | Anglo-Saxon | The people's meadow |
| Duke | | American | Nobleman |
| Duncan | | Scottish | Brown warrior |
| Dunmor | Dunmore | Scottish | Great hill fortress |
| Durand | | American | Enduring |
| Durante | | Italian | Steadfast |
| Durwin | | Anglo-Saxon | Friend of the deer |
| Durwyn | | Anglo-Saxon | Friend of the deer |
| Dustin | Dusty | Anglo-Saxon | Dusty town |
| Dwayne | | Irish | Dark |
| Dwight | | American | Wine lover |
| Dwyer | | Irish | Dark |
| Dylan | Dillon, Dylon Dillan | Welsh | Celtic god associated with the sea |

| Name | Alternate spellings | Origin | Meaning |
|---|---|---|---|

## E

| Name | Alternate spellings | Origin | Meaning |
|---|---|---|---|
| Eagle | | English | Bird of prey |
| Eamon | Eamonn, Eammon | Irish | Wealthy guardian |
| Earl | Earle | Anglo-Saxon | Nobleman |
| Ebbo | | German | Boar |
| Ebenezer | | Hebrew | Foundation stone. First name of Charles Dickens' mean-spirited *Scrooge* |
| Eberardo | | Italian | Strong as a wild boar |
| Eddison | Eddie | Anglo-Saxon | Son of Edward |
| Eden | | Hebrew | Pleasure |
| Edgar | | Anglo-Saxon | Lucky spearman |
| Edilio | | Italian | Like a statue |
| Edmondo | | Italian | Wealthy guardian |
| Edmund | Edmond | Anglo-Saxon | Prosperous protector |
| Édouard | | French | Wealthy guardian |
| Eduardo | | Italian | Wealthy guardian |
| Edward | Ted, Ed, Eddy | Anglo-Saxon | Wealthy guardian |
| Edwin | Edwyn | Anglo-Saxon | Prosperous friend |
| Efrain | | Spanish | Fruitful |
| Eldon | | Anglo-Saxon | Foreign hill |
| Eldrid | | Anglo-Saxon | Old and wise advisor |
| Eldwyn | | Anglo-Saxon | Old and wise friend |
| Elewa | | African | Intelligent |
| Eli | | American | From Elijah (The Lord is my God) |

| Name | Alternate spellings | Origin | Meaning |
|------|--------------------|--------|---------|
| Elia | Eliyah | Italian | My God is Yaweh, Biblical prophet |
| Eligio | | Italian | Chosen |
| Elijah | Elia, Eliyah | Hebrew | My God is Yaweh, Biblical prophet |
| Eliot | Elliot | Hebrew | Anglosaxon surname, adapted from Elijah |
| Ellis | | Hebrew | God is my Lord |
| Ellison | | Hebrew | God is my Lord |
| Elmer | | Anglo-Saxon | Noble |
| Elton | | Anglo-Saxon | Ella's town |
| Elvis | | Anglo-Saxon | All wise |
| Emanuele | Emmanuele | Italian | God is with us |
| Emerson | | American | Surname |
| Emil | | Latin | Ingratiating |
| Émile | | French | Rival |
| Emilio | | Italian, Spanish | Rival |
| Emir | | Arabic | Charming prince |
| Emmanuel | | Hebrew | God is with us |
| Emmet | | Anglo-Saxon | Hard working |
| Emmett | | American | Hard working, strong |
| Emrys | | Welsh | Immortal |
| Ennio | | Italian | Predestined, favoured by God |
| Enoch | | Hebrew | Teacher |
| Enrico | | Italian | Ruler of the home |
| Enrique | | Spanish | Ruler of the home |
| Erasmus | | Greek | Worthy of love |

| Name | Alternate spellings | Origin | Meaning |
|------|---------------------|--------|---------|
| Ercole | | Italian | Glory of Hera (after Hercules, mythical Greek hero) |
| Eric | | Anglo-Saxon | Eternal ruler |
| Erik | Eric, Eirik | Scandinavian | Eternal ruler |
| Erin | | Irish | From Ireland |
| Erland | | Scandinavian | Stranger |
| Ernst | | German | Serious business. Fight to the death |
| Eros | | Greek | God of love in myth, also known as Cupid |
| Errol | | Latin | To wander |
| Esme | | French | Handsome |
| Esmond | | Anglo-Saxon | Wealthy protector |
| Esteban | | Spanish | Crown |
| Etan | | Hebrew | Strong or long-lived |
| Ethan | | Hebrew | Strong or long-lived |
| Étienne | | French | Crown |
| Euan | Eoghan, Ewan | Scottish | Born of the yew |
| Eugene | | Greek | Well born |
| Eustace | | Greek | Steadfast |
| Evan | | Welsh | God is gracious |
| Evelyn | | Anglo-Saxon | Desired |
| Everley | | American | Singing |
| Evert | | German | Boar, strong, hardy |
| Ewan | Eoghan, Euan | Scottish | Born of the yew |
| Eze | | African | King |
| Ezio | | Italian | Eagle |
| Ezra | | Hebrew | Strong |

| Name | Alternate spellings | Origin | Meaning |
|------|---------------------|--------|---------|
| **F** | | | |
| Fabian | | Latin | Bean grower |
| Fabio | | Italian | Bean grower |
| Fable | | English | Story with a lesson |
| Fabrizio | | Italian | Craftsman |
| Faddei | | Russian | Heart |
| Fadil | | Arabic | The generous or distinguished one |
| Fahim | | African | Learned |
| Fairfax | | English | Warm |
| Faisal | | Arabic | A wise judge |
| Falcon | | English | Bird of prey |
| Fargo | | American | US place name |
| Farhani | | African | Happy |
| Farid | | Arabic | Unique, unrivalled |
| Farley | | Anglo-Saxon | The far meadow |
| Farook | | Arabic | One who can distinguish right from wrong |
| Farquar | Farquart | French | Masculine |
| Farrell | | Irish | Hero |
| Fausto | | Italian, Spanish | Lucky, fortunate one |
| Faustus | | Latin | Lucky, fortunate one |
| Faysal | | Arabic | A wise judge |
| Fearghal | | Irish | Brave man |
| Federico | | Italian, Spanish | Peaceful ruler |
| Fedot | | Russian | Given to God |
| Felipe | | Spanish | Horse lover |
| Felix | | Latin | Happy and prosperous |
| Feofilakt | | Russian | Guarded by God |
| Feofilart | | Russian | Guarded by God |

| Name | Alternate spellings | Origin | Meaning |
|------|---------------------|--------|---------|
| Ferapont | | Russian | Servant |
| Ferdinand | | Anglo-Saxon | Brave peacemaker |
| Ferdinando | | Italian, Spanish | Brave peacemaker |
| Ferghus | | Irish | Properous |
| Fergus | | Irish | Prosperous |
| Ferguson | | Irish | Brave, excellent |
| Fernando | | Spanish | Brave leader |
| Feroz | | Arabic | Victorious and successful |
| Ferran | | Arabic | Baker |
| Ferrari | | Italian | Italian surname meaning blacksmith, also famous supercar |
| Ferruccio | | Italian | Iron man |
| Festus | | Latin | Happy |
| Fidel | | Latin | Faithful |
| Fidenzio | | Italian | Faithful |
| Fife | | Scottish | Bright-eyed |
| Figaro | | Latin | Daring, cunning |
| Filiberto | | Italian | Illustrious |
| Filippo | | Italian | Lover of horses |
| Filius | | Latin | Son |
| Finbar | Fin, Fynbar | Irish | Fair haired |
| Findlay | Finlay, Finley | Irish, Scottish | Fair-haired hero |
| Finlay | Findlay, Finley | Irish, Scottish | Fair-haired hero |
| Finn | | Irish | Fair |
| Finnegan | | Irish | Fair |
| Fiorello | | Italian | Flourishing |
| Fiorenzo | | Italian | Flourishing |
| Firdos | | Arabic | Paradise |
| Fire | | Anglo-Saxon | Flames |
| Firenze | | Latin | City of Florence, Italy |
| Fitzgerald | | German | Son of the spear ruler |

| Name | Alternate spellings | Origin | Meaning |
|------|---------------------|--------|---------|
| Flame | | Anglo-Saxon | Flicker from a fire |
| Flannagan | | Irish | Red-head |
| Flavio | | Italian | Blonde, golden |
| Floyd | | Anglo-Saxon | Grey or white haired |
| Flynn | | Irish | Son of the red-headed man |
| Foley | | Anglo-Saxon | Creative |
| Foma | | Russian | Twin |
| Ford | | Anglo-Saxon | Lives near the ford |
| Forest | | Anglo-Saxon | Large area of trees |
| Fosco | | Italian | Dark |
| Fowler | | Anglo-Saxon | Hunter |
| Fran | | French | From Francois, Frenchman |
| Francesco | | Italian | From France |
| Francis | Frances, Fran | Latin | Free man/from France |
| Francisco | | Spanish | From France, free |
| Franco | | Italian | From France |
| François | | French | From France |
| Frank | | Anglo-Saxon | Frenchman |
| Frankie | | Latin | From France/ free man |
| Franklin | | Anglo-Saxon | Freeman who owns property |
| Franz | | German | Frenchman |
| Fraser | | French | Strawberry |
| Frasier | | French | Strawberry |
| Fred | | Anglo-Saxon | Brave peacemaker |
| Freddie | | Anglo-Saxon | Brave peacemaker |
| Frédéric | | French | Brave peacemaker |

| Name | Alternate spellings | Origin | Meaning |
|------|---------------------|--------|---------|
| Frederick | Fred, Freddie | Anglo-Saxon | Peace |
| Frederik | | German | Peace, power |
| Free | | English | At liberty |
| Freeman | | Anglo-Saxon | Free man |
| Friedrich | | German | Peace, power |
| Fritz | | German | Peace, power |
| Frode | | Scandinavian | Knowing |
| Fulbright | | German | Brilliant, bright |
| Furio | | Italian | Lively one |

| Name | Alternate spellings | Origin | Meaning |
|------|---------------------|--------|---------|
| **G** | | | |
| Gabe | | Hebrew | God is my strength |
| Gabrian | | Hebrew | God is my strength |
| Gabriel | Gabriele | Hebrew | God is my strength |
| Galen | | Greek | Calm |
| Galeno | | Spanish, Italian | From Galilee |
| Gallagher | | Irish | Helpful |
| Gallileo | | Italian | From famous scientist Gallilei Gallileo |
| Gamal | | Arabic | Camel |
| Gambero | | Spanish | Hooligan |
| Ganan | | Australian | From the west |
| Gandolfo | | Italian | Wolf, warrior |
| Ganesh | | Sanskrit | The Hindu God of wisdom |
| Garcia | | Spanish | Strong |
| Gareth | | Welsh | Gentle |
| Garsah | | Russian | Honour |
| Gary | | Welsh | Gentle |
| Gaspare | | Italian | Respected teacher |
| Gautama | | Sanskrit | The name of the Buddha |
| Gavin | | Welsh | White falcon |
| Gavriel | | Hebrew | God is my strength |
| Gavril | | Russian | Strength of God |
| Gawain | | Welsh | White falcon |
| Gelar | | Australian | A brother |
| Gene | | Greek | Noble |
| Gennadi | | Russian | Noble |
| Gennaro | | Italian | Dedicated to the God Janus |

| Name | Alternate spellings | Origin | Meaning |
|------|---------------------|--------|---------|
| Geno | | Italian | Spontaneous |
| Gentil | | Spanish | Charming |
| Geoff | | Anglo-Saxon | Peaceful |
| Geoffrey | | Anglo-Saxon | Peaceful |
| George | Jorge | Greek | Farmer |
| Georges | Jorges | Greek | From the farm |
| Georgie | | Greek | Farmer |
| Gerald | | Anglo-Saxon | Brave with a spear |
| Geraldo | | Italian | Brave with a spear |
| Gerard | | Anglo-Saxon | Brave with a spear |
| Gérard | | French | Brave with a spear |
| Gere | | English | Dramatic |
| Germain | | French | From Germany |
| Geronimo | | Italian | Sacred name. A famous Apache chief |
| Gervaise | | French | Man of honour |
| Gethin | | Welsh | Dusky |
| Ghalib | | African | Winner |
| Ghandi | | Sanskrit | Sun |
| Ghassan | | Arabic | Youthful |
| Giacomo | | Italian | He who replaces |
| Giancarlo | | Italian | God is gracious, strong |
| Gianetto | | Italian | God is gracious |
| Gianfranco | | Italian | God is gracious/ free man, from France |
| Gianni | | Italian | God is gracious |
| Gideon | | Hebrew | Tree cutter |
| Gidon | | Hebrew | Tree cutter |
| Gil | | Hebrew | Eternal joy |
| Gilderoy | | Latin | Golden king |
| Gildo | | Italian | Brave one |

| Name | Alternate spellings | Origin | Meaning |
|------|---------------------|--------|---------|
| Giles | | Greek | Young goat |
| Gili | | Hebrew | Eternal joy |
| Gillespie | | Scottish | Humble |
| Gilli | | Hebrew | Eternal joy |
| Gilroy | | Scottish | Serves the king |
| Gino | | Italian | God is gracious |
| Ginton | | Arabic | Garden |
| Giorgio | | Italian | Farmer |
| Giovanni | | Italian | God is gracious |
| Gladwyn | | Anglo-Saxon | Light of heart |
| Glen | Glenn | Scottish | Secluded valley |
| Glyn | Glynn | Welsh | Secluded valley |
| Godfrey | | German | God's peace |
| Godric | | Anglo-Saxon | Power of God |
| Goldie | | Anglo-Saxon | Precious metal |
| Gomez | | Spanish | From Spanish surname, meaning man |
| Gopal | | Sanskrit | The cowherd |
| Gordon | | Anglo-Saxon | Hill near the meadow |
| Govinda | | Sanskrit | A cowherd |
| Gowan | | Welsh | Pure |
| Graeme | Graham, Grahame | Scottish | Grand home |
| Graham | | Anglo-Saxon | Grand home |
| Grant | | Scottish | Large |
| Grégoire | | French | Watchman |
| Gregorio | | Italian | Watchman |
| Gregory | Greg, Gregor | Greek | Watchful |
| Griffin | | Greek | Mythical animal half eagle, half lion |
| Grigor | | Russian | Watchful |
| Guido | | Italian | Guide |
| Guillaume | | Anglo-Saxon | Strong protector |
| Guillermo | | Spanish | Strong protector |
| Guiseppe | | Italian | God will add |

| Name | Alternate spellings | Origin | Meaning |
|------|---------------------|--------|---------|
| Gunne | | Scandinavian | Strife |
| Gunther | | German | Army of strife |
| Gustav | | Scandinavian | Staff of the Goths |
| Guthne | | Irish | Heroic |
| Guy | | Latin | Guide |
| Gwithyen | | Cornish | From St Gwithian |

| Name | Alternate spellings | Origin | Meaning |
|------|--------------------|--------|---------|

# H

| Name | Alternate spellings | Origin | Meaning |
|------|--------------------|--------|---------|
| Haamid | | African | Grateful |
| Habib | | Arabic | The beloved one |
| Hadi | | Arabic | A guide or leader |
| Hafiz | | Arabic | The guardian |
| Hagrid | | Greek | Giant in Greek mythology |
| Hail | | Anglo-Saxon | Ice that falls like rain |
| Hakim | | Arabic | Wise and judicious |
| Haley | | Irish | Innovator |
| Halvard | | Scandinavian | Strong defender |
| Hamal | | Arabic | As gentle as a lamb |
| Hamid | | Arabic | The thankful one |
| Hamilton | | Anglo-Saxon | Grassy hill |
| Hamish | | Scottish | He who replaces |
| Hamlet | | Literary | *Hamlet* by William Shakespeare |
| Hani | | Arabic | The contented one |
| Hank | | American | Pet name for Henry, home ruler |
| Hansel | | German | God is gracious |
| Harald | | Scandinavian | Army leader |
| Hari | | Sanskrit | He who removes evil |
| Harrison | | Anglo-Saxon | Son of Harry |
| Harry | | Anglo-Saxon | Ruler of home |
| Hartley | Hartly | Anglo-Saxon | Wanderer |
| Harvey | | Scottish, Irish | Eager for battle |
| Hasim | | Arabic | The decisive one |

| Name | Alternate spellings | Origin | Meaning |
|------|---------------------|--------|---------|
| Hassan | | Arabic | Handsome |
| Havard | | Scandinavian | Strong protector |
| Hayward | | Anglo-Saxon | Keeper of the field |
| Heath | | Anglo-Saxon | Moorland |
| Hector | | Greek | To hold fast. Mythical hero of Troy |
| Heinrich | | German | Ruler of the home |
| Heinz | | German | Ruler of the home |
| Helmut | | German | Protective spirit |
| Henderson | | Anglo-Saxon | Son of Henry |
| Henri | | French | Ruler of the home |
| Henry | | Anglo-Saxon | Ruler of the home |
| Herbert | | German | Famous army |
| Hercules | | Greek | Mythical hero of immense strength |
| Hermann | | German | Army of men |
| Hermes | | Greek | Messenger of the gods |
| Hernando | | Spanish | Brave peacemaker |
| Hevan | | Hebrew | An older form of heaven |
| Hilary | Hillary | Latin | To rejoice |
| Hilton | | Anglo-Saxon | From the hill town |
| Hobart | | American | Ploughmans hill |
| Hockney | | Anglo-Saxon | Surname, notably of artist David Hockney |
| Holden | | Anglo-Saxon | Deep valley. Hero of J. D. Salinger's *Catcher in the Rye* |

| Name | Alternate spellings | Origin | Meaning |
|------|---------------------|--------|---------|
| Holder | | Anglo-Saxon | Possessor of real estate |
| Honoré | | French | Honourable |
| Hopper | | Celebrity child | (Sean Penn and Robin Wright) |
| Horace | | Latin | An hour |
| Horatio | | Latin | An hour |
| Houston | | American | US city |
| Howe | | German | High minded |
| Hubert | | German | Famous heart |
| Hugh | | Anglo-Saxon | Bright mind |
| Hugo | | German | Heart, mind, spirit |
| Humbert | | German | Famous warrior |
| Humphrey | | German | Peacemaker |
| Hurley | | Irish | Sea tide |
| Hurricane | | Anglo-Saxon | Powerful weather system |
| Hussain | Hussein | Arabic | The handsome little one |
| Huxley | | Anglo-Saxon | Outdoors man |

| Name | Alternate spellings | Origin | Meaning |
|------|---------------------|--------|---------|
| **I** | | | |
| Iago | | Spanish | The supplanter |
| Iain | | Scottish | God is gracious |
| Ian | | Scottish | God is gracious |
| Ice | | Anglo-Saxon | Frozen water |
| Ichabod | | Hebrew | Slim |
| Igor | | Russian | Bow army |
| Ilya | | Russian | Elijah |
| Imam | | Arabic | One who believes in God |
| Iman | | African | Faith |
| Immanuel | | Hebrew | God is with us |
| Indra | | Sanskrit | The God of the sky |
| Ingelbert | | German | Combative |
| Ingram | | Anglo-Saxon | Angel |
| Innis | | Irish | Isolated |
| Ioan | Euan, Ewan | Welsh | Youthful |
| Ira | | Hebrew | Cautious |
| Irwin | Irwyn | Anglo-Saxon | Sea friend |
| Isaac | | Hebrew | Laughter |
| Isidro | | Spanish | Gift of the godess Isis |
| Israel | | Hebrew | God's prince |
| Ivan | | Russian | God is gracious |
| Ivar | | Scandinavian | Archer |
| Ivor | | Anglo-Saxon | Archer's bow |
| Izaak | | Polish | Laughter |
| Izzy | | Hebrew | Friendly |

| Name | Alternate spellings | Origin | Meaning |
|---|---|---|---|
| **J** | | | |
| Jaafar | | African | Small River |
| Jabir | | Arabic | The comforter |
| Jacca | | Cornish | God is gracious |
| Jack | | Anglo-Saxon | God is gracious |
| Jackie | | Irish, Scottish | God is gracious |
| Jackson | | Anglo-Saxon | Son of Jack |
| Jacob | | Hebrew | The supplanter |
| Jacques | | French | The supplanter |
| Jaden | Jayden, Jadon, Jaydon | Hebrew | God has heard |
| Jagdish | | Sanskrit | The ruler of the world |
| Jagger | | Anglo-Saxon | Carter |
| Jago | | Cornish | The supplanter |
| Jaguar | | Spanish | Fast |
| Jaimie | | Anglo-Saxon | The supplanter |
| Jake | | Hebrew | The supplanter |
| Jaleel | | Arabic | Great |
| Jalil | | Arabic | Majestic |
| Jamal | | Arabic | The handsome one |
| James | Jamie | Anglo-Saxon | The supplanter |
| Jared | | Hebrew | Descending |
| Jarrah | | Australian | A type of tree |
| Jarrett | | Hebrew | Confident |
| Jarvis | | Anglo-Saxon | Servant with a spear |
| Jason | | Greek | Healer. Also mythical Greek hero |
| Jasper | | Anglo-Saxon | Semi-precious red gem |
| Java | | Place name | Indonesian island |
| Javier | | Spanish | The new house |
| Jaycee | | American | From the initials J. C. |

| Name | Alternate spellings | Origin | Meaning |
|------|---------------------|--------|---------|
| Jayden | Jaydon, Jaden, Jadon | Hebrew | God has heard |
| Jazz | | American | Short for Jason or Jasper |
| Jean | | French | God is gracious |
| Jedadiah | Jed, Jedd | Hebrew | Beloved by God |
| Jedd | | Hebrew | Beloved by God |
| Jedi | | Hebrew | Beloved by God |
| Jefferson | | American | Son of Jeffrey |
| Jeffrey | Geoffrey | Anglo-Saxon | Peaceful |
| Jem | Jemmy | Literary | *To Kill a Mockingbird* by Harper Lee, *Jamaica Inn* by Daphne DuMaurier |
| Jerara | | Australian | Falling water |
| Jeremiah | | Hebrew | God will uplift |
| Jeremias | | Spanish | God will uplift |
| Jeremy | Jez, Jem | Anglo-Saxon | God will uplift |
| Jermaine | | French | Brother |
| Jermajesty | | Celebrity child | (Jermaine Jackson) |
| Jerome | | Greek | Sacred name |
| Jerral | | American | From Gerald |
| Jerrett | | Hebrew | Confident |
| Jesse | Jess | Hebrew | Wealthy/God's gift |
| Jesus | | Hebrew | Jehova is salvation |
| Jet | | Latin | Black |
| Jethro | | Hebrew | Overflowing or abundance |
| Jevon | | Anglo-Saxon | Young |
| Jim | Jimmy | Anglo-Saxon | Short for James. He who replaces |
| Jirra | | Australian | A kangaroo |
| Jitender | | Sanskrit | The powerful conqueror |

| Name | Alternate spellings | Origin | Meaning |
|------|---------------------|--------|---------|
| Joe | Jo | Hebrew | Usually short for Joseph, God shall add |
| Joachim | | Hebrew | Established by God |
| Joaquim | | Hebrew | Established by God |
| Jock | | Scottish | God is gracious |
| Joe | | Hebrew | Shortened version of Joseph |
| Joel | | Hebrew | The Lord is God |
| Johanne | Johan, Johannes | Scandinavian | God is gracious |
| John | | Hebrew | God is gracious |
| Jon | | Hebrew | God is gracious |
| Jonah | | Hebrew | Dove |
| Jonas | | Hebrew | Dove |
| Jonathan | Jonathon | Hebrew | Gift of God |
| Jonte | | American | God is gracious |
| Jools | Jules | Anglo-Saxon | Young |
| Jordan | | Hebrew | To flow down or descend |
| Jorell | | American | Mighty spearman |
| Jorge | | Spanish | Farmer |
| Jose | | Spanish | God will add |
| Joseph | | Hebrew | God will add |
| Josh | | Hebrew | God is salvation |
| Joshua | | Hebrew | God is salvation |
| Joss | | Hebrew | God is salvation |
| Jove | | Latin | Roman god of the sky |
| Jowan | | Cornish | God is gracious |
| Juan | | Spanish | God is gracious |
| Jud | | Hebrew | Praised |
| Judas | | Hebrew | Praised. Disciple who betrayed Christ |

| Name | Alternate spellings | Origin | Meaning |
|------|--------------------|---------|---------|
| Judd | Jud | Latin | Secretive |
| Jude | | Hebrew | Praised |
| Judge | | English | To form an opinion, or person who presides over a court of law |
| Jules | | Latin | Youthful |
| Julian | Julien | French | Youthful |
| Julius | | Latin | Youthful |
| Justin | | Latin | Just or true |
| Justus | | Latin | Fair |
| Jyotis | | Sanskrit | Light |

| Name | Alternate spellings | Origin | Meaning |
|------|---------------------|--------|---------|

## K

| Name | Alternate spellings | Origin | Meaning |
|------|---------------------|--------|---------|
| Kacy | | American | From Casey |
| Kadin | | Arabic | Friend |
| Kadir | | Arabic | Powerful |
| Kai | | Pacific Islands | Good looking |
| Kale | | American | Healthy |
| Kalid | | Arabic | Eternal |
| Kalil | | Arabic | Good friend |
| Kama | | Sanskrit | The golden one |
| Kamal | | Arabic | Perfect |
| Kamil | | Arabic | Perfect |
| Kane | | Irish | Tribute |
| Karan | | Sanskrit | A warrior |
| Kari | | Australian | Smoke |
| Karim | | Arabic | Noble and generous |
| Karl | | Russian | Manly |
| Karl | | German | Free man |
| Karsten | | German | Christian |
| Kasey | | Irish | Brave |
| Kasim | | Arabic | One who shares or distributes |
| Kaspar | | Scandinavian | From the semi-precious gem, Jasper |
| Kateb | | Arabic | Scribe |
| Kauri | | Pacific Islands | A kind of tree |
| Kay | | Welsh | Joy |
| Kazimir | | Russian | To destroy greatness |
| Keagan | | Irish | Little fire |
| Kean | | Irish | Handsome |
| Keanan | | Irish | Ancient |
| Keane | | German | Attractive |
| Keanu | | Pacific Islands | Cool breeze over the mountain |
| Kearney | | Irish | Sparkling |

| Name | Alternate spellings | Origin | Meaning |
|------|--------------------|--------|---------|
| Keats | | Literary | Surname of the romantic poet |
| Kedar | | Arabic | Powerful |
| Keefe | | Irish | Handsome |
| Keegan | | Irish | Little fire |
| Keenan | | Irish | Ancient |
| Keith | | Welsh | Of the forest |
| Kelly | | Irish | Warrior |
| Kelsey | | Scandinavian | Unique |
| Kelvin | | Irish | From the narrow river |
| Kemal | | Arabic | Perfect |
| Ken | | Irish | Handsome |
| Kendall | | Anglo-Saxon | Shy |
| Kendrick | | Irish | Royal ruler |
| Kennedy | | Irish | Ugly head. Surname of US President, John F. Kennedy |
| Kenneth | | Irish | Handsome |
| Kent | | Place name | English county |
| Kent | | Welsh | Bright |
| Keoni | | Pacific Islands | The righteous one |
| Kevern | | Cornish | From St Kevern |
| Kevin | | Irish | Little gentle one |
| Khalid | | Arabic | Eternal |
| Khalif | | Arabic | Successor |
| Khalil | | Arabic | A friend |
| Kid | | American | Slang for child |
| Kieran | | Irish | Little dark one |
| Kim | | Anglo-Saxon | Warrior chief |
| King | | Anglo-Saxon | Ruler |
| Kingsley | | Anglo-Saxon | From the king's meadow |
| Kipp | | Anglo-Saxon | From the pointed hill |
| Kiran | | Sanskrit | A ray of light |

| Name | Alternate spellings | Origin | Meaning |
|------|---------------------|--------|---------|
| Kirby | | Anglo-Saxon | From the church town |
| Kirwyn | | Welsh | Dark skinned |
| Kit | | Greek | Bearer of Christ |
| Klaud | | Latin | The lame one |
| Knox | | Anglo-Saxon | Bold |
| Knut | | Scandinavian | Knot, a short, stout man |
| Kofi | | African | Born on Friday. First name of Nobel Peace Prize winner, Kofi Anan |
| Kolet | | Australian | A dove |
| Kolya | | Russian | Victory of the people |
| Konrad | | German | Brave advisor |
| Koorong | | Australian | A canoe |
| Kosey | | African | Lion |
| Krishna | | Sanskrit | Dark, black |
| Krispin | Krispen | Latin | Curly haired |
| Kristian | | Scandinavian | Follower of Christ |
| Kristopher | | Greek | Bearer of Christ |
| Kulan | | Australian | A possom |
| Kumar | | Sanskrit | Boy |
| Kupe | | Pacific Islands | A heroic explorer |
| Kurt | | German | Brave advisor |
| Kyd | | Celebrity child | (David Duchovny and Tea Leoni) |
| Kyle | | Scottish | Narrow channel |
| Kyzer | | American | Wild spirit |

| Name | Alternate spellings | Origin | Meaning |
|------|---------------------|--------|---------|
| **L** | | | |
| Lacy | | Latin | From the Roman villa |
| Lai | | Sanskrit | The beloved one |
| Lakshman | | Sanskrit | Lucky |
| Lamberto | | Italian | Famous in his country |
| Lance | | Anglo-Saxon | Knight's attendant |
| Lando | | Italian | Land, earth |
| Lane | | Anglo-Saxon | From a narrow lane |
| Langley | | Anglo-Saxon | Lives by a meadow |
| Lani | | Pacific Islands | The sky |
| Larry | | Latin | Crowned with laurels |
| Latif | | Arabic | Kind and gentle |
| Laurence | | Latin | Crowned with laurels |
| Laurent | | French | Crowned with laurels |
| Laurie | | Latin | Crowned with laurels |
| Lawrence | | Latin | Crowned with laurels |
| Leaf | | Anglo-Saxon | Foliage |
| Leander | | Greek | The lion man |
| Lee | | Anglo-Saxon | From the meadow |
| Leighton | | Anglo-Saxon | From the meadow farm |
| Leith | | Scottish | Wide river |
| Lemony | | Literature | From 'Lemony Snicket': pen name of author of *A Series of Unfortunate Events* |

| Name | Alternate spellings | Origin | Meaning |
|------|---------------------|--------|---------|
| Lennon | | Irish | Lover, sweetheart |
| Lennox | | Scottish | From the place of many elm trees |
| Leo | | Italian | Lion |
| Leo | | Latin | A lion |
| Léon | | Latin | Like a lion |
| Leonardo | | Italian, Spanish | Like a lion |
| Leone | | Italian | Lion |
| Leopold | | Italian | He who is distinguished |
| Leroy | | French | The king |
| Lesley | Leslie | Scottish | From the grey fortress |
| Lestat | | Literary | *Vampire Chronicles* by Anne Rice |
| Lester | | Anglo-Saxon | From the army camp |
| Levi | | Hebrew | Joined or united |
| Lewis | | Anglo-Saxon | Famous fighter |
| Lewyth | | Cornish | Ruler |
| Liam | | Irish | Strong protector |
| Liberio | | Italian | Independant |
| Libero | | Italian | Independant |
| Lincoln | | Welsh | Lake on a hill ridge. Name of US President, Abraham Lincoln |
| Lindsey | | Anglo-Saxon | Lincoln's marsh |
| Linford | | Anglo-Saxon | From the lime tree ford |
| Linus | | Greek | Blonde haired |
| Lionel | | Latin | A lion |
| Lisandro | | Italian | Free man |
| Ljluka | | Sanskrit | An owl |

| Name | Alternate spellings | Origin | Meaning |
|------|---------------------|--------|---------|
| Llewelyn | | Welsh | Like a lion |
| Lloyd | | Welsh | Grey hair |
| Logan | | Irish | Lives by the hollow |
| London | | Place name | Capital of the UK |
| Lorenzo | | Italian | From Laurentum |
| Lorimer | | Latin | Home is water |
| Louis | | French | Famous fighter |
| Lowan | | Australian | A type of bird |
| Luc | | French | Born in the light |
| Luca | | Italian | Born in the light |
| Lucas | | French | Born in the light |
| Lucian | | Latin | Born in the light |
| Luciano | | Italian | Born in the light |
| Lucio | | Italian | Born in the light |
| Lucio | | Spanish | Born in the light |
| Lucius | | Latin | Born in the light |
| Ludo | | Latin | I play |
| Ludwig | | German | Famous warrior |
| Luigi | | Italian | Famous fighter |
| Luis | | Spanish | Famous fighter |
| Luka | | Russian | From Luke |
| Luke | | Greek | Born in the light. One of Christ's apostles |
| Lupus | | Latin | Wolf, a constellation |
| Luther | | German | People's army |
| Lyle | | Scottish | Loyal |
| Lyman | Leyman | Anglo-Saxon | From the meadow |
| Lyndon | | Anglo-Saxon | Lives by the linden tree |
| Lynn | | Welsh | From the waterfall |

| Name | Alternate spellings | Origin | Meaning |
|------|---------------------|--------|---------|
| Lynshawn | | American | Lyn and Shawn |
| Lyon | | Place name | French city |
| Lyov | | Russian | Lion |
| Lysander | | Greek | The liberator |
| Lyulf | | German | Combative |

| Name | Alternate spellings | Origin | Meaning |
|------|---------------------|--------|---------|
| **M** | | | |
| Maalik | | African | Experienced |
| Mac | | Scottish, Irish | Son |
| Mack | | Scottish, Irish | Son |
| Mackenzie | | Scottish, Irish | Son of Coinnich 'comely' |
| Macy | | French | Weapon |
| Maddox | | Welsh | Benefactor's son |
| Magic | | English | An extraordinary or mystical influence |
| Magnus | | Greek | The great one |
| Mahatma | | Sanskrit | Great soul |
| Mahendra | | Sanskrit | The God of the sky |
| Mahesh | | Sanskrit | A great ruler |
| Mahmood | | Arabic | Praiseworthy |
| Mahomet | | Arabic | Praiseworthy |
| Mahoney | | Irish | Bear |
| Majid | | Arabic | The illustrious one |
| Maka | | Australian | A camp fire |
| Malcolm | | Scottish | Servant |
| Malik | | Arabic | The master or king |
| Mallory | | Anglo-Saxon | Military advisor |
| Malone | | Irish | Church-goer |
| Mandela | | African | Name of Nobel Peace Prize winner, Nelson Mandela |
| Manfred | | Anglo-Saxon | Peaceful hero |
| Mani | | Sanskrit | A gem |
| Mansoor | | Arabic | Victorious |
| Manu | | Pacific Islands | Man of the birds |
| Manuel | | Italian, Spanish | God is with us |

| Name | Alternate spellings | Origin | Meaning |
|------|--------------------|--------|---------|
| Marama | | Pacific Islands | Moon man |
| Marc | | Latin | From Mars God of War, warrior |
| Marcel | | French | From Mars God of War |
| Marcello | | Italian | From Mars God of War |
| Marco | | Italian, Spanish | From Mars God of War |
| Marcus | | Latin | From Mars God of War, warrior |
| Mariano | | Italian | Devoted to the Virgin Mary |
| Mario | | Italian | Devoted to the Virgin Mary |
| Mark | | Latin | From Mars God of War, warrior |
| Marley | | Anglo-Saxon | Pleasant wood |
| Marlon | | Anglo-Saxon | Little hawk |
| Marmion | | French | A monkey, brat |
| Marron | | Australian | A leaf |
| Martin | Martyn | Latin | From Mars God of War, warrior |
| Martino | | Italian | Warrior |
| Marvin | Marvyn | Anglo-Saxon | Lives by the sea |
| Massimo | | Italian | Large |
| Masud | | Arabic | The fortunate one |
| Matareka | | Pacific Islands | One with a smiling face |
| Matari | | Australian | A man |
| Matthew | Mathew | Hebrew | Gift of Jehova |
| Matthieu | | French | Gift of Jehova |
| Maui | | Pacific Islands | Legendary hero |
| Maurice | | Latin | Dark skinned, Moorish |
| Maverick | | American | A rebel |
| Mawgan | | Cornish | Mighty prince |

| Name | Alternate spellings | Origin | Meaning |
|------|--------------------|--------|---------|
| Maxwell | | Anglo-Saxon | Lives by the spring |
| Mayer | | Latin | Greater |
| Maynard | | Anglo-Saxon | Exceptionally brave and strong |
| McCartney | | Scottish | Son of Cartney |
| Melbourne | | Anglo-Saxon | From the mill stream |
| Melville | | French | Mill town |
| Melvin | | Irish | Armoured chief |
| Memphis | | Place name | US city |
| Meredith | | Welsh | Protector from the sea |
| Merlin | | Welsh | Sea hill |
| Merrill | | French | Little famous one |
| Merton | | Anglo-Saxon | Sea town |
| Michael | Mike | Hebrew | Who is like God |
| Michel | | French | In God's likeness |
| Michelangelo | | Italian | Like God, an angel |
| Micky | Mickey | Hebrew | Who is like God |
| Miguel | | Spanish | Like God |
| Mikhail | | Russian | Like God |
| Mikula | | Russian | Victory of the people |
| Milan | | Place name | Italian city |
| Milburn | | Anglo-Saxon | Mill stream |
| Miles | | Latin | A soldier |
| Milton | | Anglo-Saxon | Mill town |
| Minty | | American | From the herb, mint |
| Misha | | Russian | Like God |
| Mohammed | | Arabic | The praised one |
| Mohan | | Sanskrit | The bewitching one |
| Mohinder | | Sanskrit | The God of the sky |

| Name | Alternate spellings | Origin | Meaning |
|------|---------------------|--------|---------|
| Money | | American | Cash |
| Monroe | | Irish, Scottish | Mouth of the River Rotha |
| Montana | | Place name | US state |
| Montgomery | | Anglo-Saxon | From the wealthy man's mountain |
| Monti | | Australian | A stork |
| Moore | | French | Dark stranger |
| Morell | | French | Secretive |
| Morgan | | Scottish | Sea warrior |
| Morris | | Latin | Dark skinned, Moorish |
| Morrissey | | Anglo-Saxon | Choice of the sea |
| Morten | | Scandinavian | Warrior |
| Morton | | Anglo-Saxon | Town by the moor |
| Moses | | Hebrew | Drawn from water |
| Moswen | | African | Pale |
| Mowan | | Australian | The sun |
| Mubarak | | Arabic | Fortunate |
| Muhammad | Muhammed, Mohammed | Arabic | The praised one |
| Mukhtar | | Arabic | The chosen one |
| Mundungus | | Latin | Rubbish |
| Mungo | | Scottish | Lovable |
| Murdoch | | Scottish | Sea farer |
| Murray | | Scottish | Lord of the sea |
| Muzio | | Italian | Silent, quiet |
| Myles | | Latin | A soldier |
| Mylo | | Latin | A soldier |

| Name | Alternate spellings | Origin | Meaning |
|------|--------------------|--------|---------|
| **N** | | | |
| Naasir | | African | Defender |
| Nabil | | Arabic | Noble |
| Nadir | | Arabic | Precious, rare |
| Nambur | | Australian | A tea tree |
| Nanda | | Sanskrit | Joy |
| Nanji | | African | Safe |
| Napolean | | German | Domineering |
| Narayan | | Sanskrit | The son of man |
| Narciso | | Italian | Self love |
| Nardu | | Australian | A type of plant |
| Narendra | | Sanskrit | The mighty man |
| Narrah | | Australian | The sea |
| Nasir | | Arabic | The helper |
| Nassir | | Arabic | Protector |
| Nassor | | African | Victorious |
| Nat | | Hebrew | The gift of God |
| Natal | | Spanish | Born at Christmas |
| Nathan | | Hebrew | The gift of God |
| Navarro | | Spanish | Wild spirit |
| Neal | Neale | Irish | Champion |
| Ned | | Anglo-Saxon | Wealthy guardian |
| Neil | | Scottish | Champion |
| Nellie | | Anglo-Saxon | Short for Nelson, singing |
| Nelson | | English | Son of Neil |
| Nemo | | Latin | No name, nobody |
| Neo | | Greek | New |
| Nereo | | Italian | Great swimmer |
| Nero | | Latin | Dark |
| Neron | | Spanish | Strong |
| Nestor | | Greek | Wisdom |
| Nevada | | Spanish | Snow-capped |

| Name | Alternate spellings | Origin | Meaning |
|------|--------------------|--------|---------|
| Neville | | French | From the new town |
| Newbie | | American | Beginner |
| Newlin | | Welsh | Able |
| Newton | | Anglo-Saxon | From the new town |
| Niall | | Irish | Champion |
| Nicholas | Nick, Nicky, Nicolas | Greek | Victory of the people |
| Nick | | Greek | Victory of the people |
| Nicolas | | French | Victory of the people |
| Niels | Nils | Scandinavian | Victory of the people |
| Nigel | | Latin | Dark, black haired |
| Nike | | Greek | Winning |
| Nikita | | Russian | Unconquearble |
| Niklaus | | Scandinavian | Victory of the people |
| Nikolai | | Russian | Victory of the people |
| Nimrod | | Latin | Valiant/great hunter |
| Nino | | Italian | Handsome |
| Nioka | | Australian | Hills |
| Nirvana | | Sanskrit | In Buddhism, Nirvana is a blissful spiritual state of clarity and compassion |
| Nissan | | Hebrew | Omen |
| Nixon | | Anglo-Saxon | Audacious |
| Noah | | Hebrew | Rest, peace |
| Noe | | French | Rest, peace |
| Noël | | French | Christmas |
| Nolan | | Irish | Noble |

| Name | Alternate spellings | Origin | Meaning |
|---|---|---|---|
| Norbert | | German | Famous one from the north |
| Nordin | | Scandinavian | Handsome |
| Norman | | Anglo-Saxon | Norseman |
| Norton | | Anglo-Saxon | From the north town |
| Norville | | French | Northern town |
| Norward | | Anglo-Saxon | Guardian of the north |
| Nuri | | Arabic | Fire |
| Nyle | Niall | Irish | Champion |

| Name | Alternate spellings | Origin | Meaning |
|------|--------------------|---------|---------|

## O

| Name | Alternate spellings | Origin | Meaning |
|------|--------------------|---------|---------|
| Oakley | | Anglo-Saxon | From the oak meadow |
| Oberon | | Literary | *A Midsummer Night's Dream* by William Shakespeare |
| Ocean | | Greek | Immense |
| Ochre | | English | Brown, yellow |
| Octavius | | Latin | The eighth born |
| Odin | | Anglo-Saxon | God of all |
| Odongo | | African | Second of twins |
| Ogden | | Anglo-Saxon | From the oak valley |
| Ola | | Scandinavian | Ancestor, heir |
| Olaf | | Scandinavian | Ancestor, heir |
| Oleg | | Russian | Successful |
| Olindo | | Italian | From Olinthos |
| Oliver | | Latin | Of the olive tree, peaceful |
| Olivero | | Italian | Olive tree |
| Olivier | | French | Olive tree |
| Oman | | Scandinavian | High protector |
| Omar | | Arabic | First born son |
| Omero | | Italian | Known for his land holdings |
| Onslow | | Anglo-Saxon | A hasty man's hill |
| Ora | | Pacific Islands | Life |
| Orad | | Australian | Earth |
| Oreste | | Italian | Mountain man |
| Orin | | Hebrew | Tree |
| Orion | | Greek | The hunter. A constellation |
| Orlando | Orly | Italian, Spanish | Gives glory to his country |

| Name | Alternate spellings | Origin | Meaning |
|------|--------------------|--------|---------|
| Orme | | Anglo-Saxon | Kind |
| Oroiti | | Pacific Islands | Slow-footed one |
| Oronzo | | Italian | Swift, agile |
| Orran | | Irish | Green-eyed |
| Orsen | | Latin | Little bear |
| Orso | | Italian | Bear |
| Ortensio | | Italian | Gardener |
| Orvin | | Anglo-Saxon | Brave friend |
| Orvyn | | Anglo-Saxon | Brave friend |
| Osborne | | Anglo-Saxon | Soldier of God |
| Osburt | | Anglo-Saxon | Smart |
| Oscar | | Italian | Warrior of God |
| Osgood | | Anglo-Saxon | A good man |
| Osman | | Arabic | A servant of God |
| Osmond | | Anglo-Saxon | Divine protection |
| Oswald | | Anglo-Saxon | Divine power |
| Othello | | Spanish | Bold |
| Otis | | Greek | Keen of hearing |
| Otto | | German | Wealthy |
| Ottone | | Italian | Owner |
| Ovidio | | Italian | Cattle owner |
| Owen | | Welsh | Noble |
| Ox | | American | Strong |
| Oz | | Hebrew | Scholar, he who excels |

| Name | Alternate spellings | Origin | Meaning |
|------|---------------------|--------|---------|
| **P** | | | |
| Pablo | | Spanish | Small. Name of famous artist, Pablo Picasso |
| Paciano | | Italian | Man of peace |
| Pacifico | | Spanish | Man of peace |
| Paddy | | Latin | Noble, well born |
| Paki | | African | Witness |
| Pal | | Scandinavian | Small |
| Palladin | | Greek | Confrontational |
| Palmer | | Anglo-Saxon | Open |
| Palmiro | | Italian | Excellent |
| Pancho | | Spanish | From France |
| Paolo | | Italian, Spanish | Small |
| Par | | Greek | God of the forest and shepherds |
| Paris | | Greek | Mythical prince who fell in love with Helen of Troy |
| Parker | | Anglo-Saxon | Park keeper |
| Pascal | | Latin | Born at Easter |
| Pasha | | Russian | Small |
| Pat | | Latin | Noble, well born |
| Patrick | | Latin | Noble, well born |
| Patton | | Anglo-Saxon | Brash |
| Paul | | Latin | Small |
| Pavel | | Russian | Small |
| Pax | | Latin | Peace |
| Paxton | | Anglo-Saxon | From the warrior's estate |
| Pearson | | Anglo-Saxon | Son of Piers |

| Name | Alternate spellings | Origin | Meaning |
|------|---------------------|--------|---------|
| Pedro | | Spanish | Rock |
| Pele | | Hebrew | Miracle |
| Pepe | | Spanish | God shall add |
| Percival | | French | He who pierces the valley. In legend the knight who glimpsed the Holy Grail |
| Percy | | French | He who pierces the valley |
| Peregrine | | Latin | Stranger or pilgrim |
| Perry | | American | Rock |
| Peter | | Greek | Rock. One of Christ's disciples |
| Petya | | Russian | Rock |
| Philip | | Greek | Lover of horses |
| Philippe | | French | Lover of horses |
| Philo | | Greek | Loving, friendly |
| Phineas | | Latin | An oracle |
| Phoenix | | Greek | Legendary bird returns to life from ashes |
| Piero | | Italian | Rock |
| Pierre | | French | Rock |
| Piers | | Greek | Rock |
| Pietro | | Italian | Rock |
| Pindan | | Australian | Desert |
| Pio | | Italian | Pious, honest |
| Pip | | Greek | Short for Phillip |
| Piper | | Anglo-Saxon | Pipe or flute player |
| Piran | | Cornish | Prayer. Patron Saint of Cornwall |
| Pitney | | Scandinavian | Protector of the island |

| Name | Alternate spellings | Origin | Meaning |
|------|---------------------|--------|---------|
| Placido | | Italian | Calm, tranquil |
| Placido | | Latin | Calm, quiet |
| Polaris | | Latin | The north star, used as a guide by navigators |
| Pollock | | Anglo-Saxon | A fish. Surname of famous artist, Jackson Pollock |
| Powys | | Place name | Region in Wales |
| Prakash | | Sanskrit | Light, or famous |
| Prasad | | Sanskrit | Brightness |
| Prem | | Sanskrit | Love |
| Presley | | Anglo-Saxon | Priest's meadow |
| Preston | | Anglo-Saxon | Priest's town |
| Primo | | Latin | First |
| Prince | | Latin | First in rank |
| Prospero | | Italian | Happy, content, lucky |

| Name | Alternate spellings | Origin | Meaning |
|------|---------------------|--------|---------|
| **Q** | | | |
| Qabil | | Arabic | Able |
| Qadir | | Arabic | Powerful |
| Qasim | | Arabic | One who shares |
| Quasim | | Arabic | One who shares |
| Quentin | | Latin | Fifth |
| Quigley | | Scottish, Irish | One with messy hair |
| Quimby | | Scandinavian | Estate of the woman |
| Quincy | | Latin | Fifth |
| Quinlan | | Scottish | Well built |
| Quinn | | Irish | Fifth |

| Name | Alternate spellings | Origin | Meaning |
|------|--------------------|--------|---------|

# R

| Name | Alternate spellings | Origin | Meaning |
|------|--------------------|--------|---------|
| Radko | | Russian | Happy |
| Radley | | Anglo-Saxon | Red meadow |
| Radosalve | | Russian | Happy glory |
| Rafael | | Spanish | God has healed |
| Rafferty | | Irish, Scottish | Prosperous one |
| Rafi | | Arabic | The exalted one |
| Rafiki | | African | Friend |
| Rafiq | | Arabic | Friend |
| Ragnar | | Scandinavian | Military advisor |
| Rahman | | Arabic | Merciful |
| Raimondo | | Italian | Wise defender |
| Raj | | Sanskrit | King |
| Rajendra | | Sanskrit | A mighty king |
| Rajiv | | Sanskrit | Striped |
| Ralph | | Anglo-Saxon | Wolf counsellor |
| Ramesh | | Sanskrit | Ruler of Rama |
| Ramiro | | Italian, Spanish | Famous advisor |
| Ramon | | Spanish | Wise defender |
| Ramsey | | Anglo-Saxon | From the ram's island |
| Randolf | | Anglo-Saxon | Wolf shield |
| Randolph | | Anglo-Saxon | Wolf shield |
| Randy | | Anglo-Saxon | Wolf shield |
| Rangi | | Pacific Islands | Heaven |
| Ranjit | | Sanskrit | The delighted one |
| Raphael | | Hebrew | God has healed |
| Rashad | | African | Righteous |
| Rashid | | Arabic | The well-guided one |
| Rasul | | African | Messenger |
| Rata | | Pacific Islands | A great chief |
| Rauf | | Arabic | The compassionate one |

| Name | Alternate spellings | Origin | Meaning |
|------|---------------------|--------|---------|
| Raul | | Italian | Advisor, wolf |
| Raven | | English | Large, black bird |
| Ravi | | Sanskrit | Of the sun |
| Ray | | French | The sovereign |
| Raymond | | French | Wise defender |
| Reagan | | Irish | Little king |
| Rebel | | Latin | Rebellious one |
| Red | | Anglo-Saxon | A primary colour |
| Redford | | Anglo-Saxon | Red ford |
| Reece | | Welsh | In love with life |
| Reeve | | Anglo-Saxon | Steward |
| Regan | | Irish | Little king |
| Regulus | | Latin | The brightest star in the Leo constellation |
| Rehgan | | Irish | Little king |
| Reid | | Scottish | Red-head |
| Remington | | American | English surname, raven family town |
| Remus | | Latin | Fast. One of the brothers who founded Rome |
| Rémy | | French | Oarsman |
| Renaldo | | Spanish | Advisor to the king |
| Renato | | Italian | Reborn |
| René | | French | Reborn |
| Renoir | | French | Name of famous artist, Pierre Auguste Renoir |
| Reuben | Ruben, Rubin | Hebrew | Behold a son |
| Rewan | | Cornish | From St Rewan |
| Rex | | Latin | A king |
| Rhett | | Welsh | Keen |
| Rhodes | | Place name | Greek island |

| Name | Alternate spellings | Origin | Meaning |
|------|---------------------|--------|---------|
| Rhys | | Welsh | Hero |
| Ricardo | | Italian | Brave leader |
| Richard | | Anglo-Saxon | Brave leader |
| Rico | | Spanish | Brave leader |
| Ridgley | | Anglo-Saxon | From the ridge meadow |
| Riley | | Irish | Brave |
| Rinaldo | | Italian | Advisor to the king |
| Rio | | Place name | Brazilian city |
| Ripley | Rypley | Anglo-Saxon | Lives in the noisy meadow |
| Ripper | | American | |
| Ripple | | Anglo-Saxon | Disturbance in smooth water |
| Roald | | Scandinavian | Famous ruler |
| Roark | Roarke | Irish | Famous ruler |
| Roary | | Irish | Fiery, red haired |
| Robert | | Anglo-Saxon | Bright fame |
| Robert | | German | Bright fame |
| Roberto | | Italian | Bright fame |
| Robin | Robyn | Anglo-Saxon | Bright fame |
| Robson | | Anglo-Saxon | Son of Robert |
| Rocco | | Italian | Rest |
| Rochester | | Anglo-Saxon | Camp on the rocks |
| Rock | | Anglo-Saxon | Large stone |
| Rocky | | Anglo-Saxon | Large stones |
| Roderick | | Anglo-Saxon | Famous power |
| Roderigo | | Spanish | Famous power |
| Rodolfo | | Italian, Spanish | Famous wolf |
| Rodrigo | | Italian, Spanish | Famous power |
| Rogelio | | Spanish | Request |
| Roger | | German | Famous spearman |

| Name | Alternate spellings | Origin | Meaning |
|------|---------------------|--------|---------|
| Roland | | Anglo-Saxon | Famous in the land |
| Roland | | German | Famous land |
| Rolando | | Italian | Famous in the land |
| Rolf | | German | Famous wolf |
| Roman | | Anglo-Saxon | From Rome |
| Romano | | Italian | From Rome |
| Romeo | | Latin | Pilgrim to Rome. Name of Shakespeare's tragic lover in *Romeo and Juliet* |
| Romney | | Welsh | Curving river |
| Romolo | | Italian | Lives near a river |
| Ronald | | Scottish | Rules with good judgement |
| Ronan | | Irish | Little seal |
| Rongo | | Pacific Islands | God of rain |
| Rooney | | Scottish | The red one |
| Rorke | | Irish | Famous ruler |
| Rory | | German | Red ruler |
| Ross | | Scottish | Lives on the headland |
| Rothwell | | Scandinavian | From the red well |
| Rowan | | Anglo-Saxon | Kind of tree with berries |
| Roy | | French | King |
| Royce | | Anglo-Saxon | Son of the king |
| Royston | | Anglo-Saxon | Town of Royce |
| Ruben | Reuben, Rubin | Hebrew | Behold a son |
| Rubeus | | Greek | Red |
| Rubin | | Hebrew | Behold a son |
| Rudd | | Anglo-Saxon | Ruddy complexion |

| Name | Alternate spellings | Origin | Meaning |
|------|--------------------|--------|---------|
| Rudi | | German | Famous wolf |
| Rudolf | | German | Famous wolf |
| Ruel | | Hebrew | Friend of God |
| Rufino | | Italian | Red haired |
| Rufus | | Latin | Red haired |
| Rune | | Scandinavian | Secret lore |
| Rupert | | German | Bright fame |
| Rurik | | Russian | Famous power |
| Russell | | Anglo-Saxon | Red haired |
| Rusty | | Anglo-Saxon | Pet name for Russell |
| Rutledge | | Anglo-Saxon | From the red pool |
| Ryan | | Irish | Little king |
| Ryder | | Celebrity child | (Kate Hudson) |

| Name | Alternate spellings | Origin | Meaning |
|------|--------------------|--------|---------|
| **S** | | | |
| Saad | | African | Good fortune |
| Sabir | | Arabic | The patient one |
| Sadik | | Arabic | Truthful, or faithful |
| Saeed | | African | Lucky |
| Saggitarius | | Latin | The archer. Star sign and constellation |
| Said | | African | Happy |
| Salaam | | African | Peace |
| Salado | | Spanish | Amusing |
| Salah | | Arabic | Good, righteous |
| Salazar | | Latin | Palace |
| Salim | | Arabic | Safe |
| Salman | | Arabic | Protector |
| Saloman | | Hebrew | Peaceful |
| Salvador | | Spanish | Saviour |
| Salvatore | | Italian | Saviour |
| Salvo | | Italian | Saviour |
| Sam | | Hebrew | Asked of God |
| Sampson | | Hebrew | Of the sun, or strong man |
| Samson | | Hebrew | Of the sun, or strong man |
| Samuel | | Hebrew | Asked of God |
| Samuele | | Italian | Asked of God |
| Sancho | | Spanish | Saintly |
| Sanders | | Anglo-Saxon | From Alexander, defender of mankind |
| Sandy | Sandie | Greek | Defender of mankind |
| Sanford | | Anglo-Saxon | Negotiator |
| Sanjay | | Sanskrit | Triumphant |
| Sankara | | Sanskrit | Lucky |
| Sante | | Italian | Saintly |

| Name | Alternate spellings | Origin | Meaning |
|------|--------------------|--------|---------|
| Santiago | | Spanish | St James |
| Santo | | Italian | Saintly |
| Santos | | Spanish | Saintly |
| Sarni | | Arabic | The elevated one |
| Sasha | | Russian | Defender of mankind |
| Satchel | | Latin | Small bag |
| Saul | | Hebrew | Asked for or prayed for |
| Saverio | | Italian | Luminous |
| Saville | | French | Stylish |
| Sawyer | | Literary | *The Adventures of Tom Sawyer* by Mark Twain |
| Saxon | | Anglo-Saxon | Germanic people |
| Sayed | | Arabic | The lord, the master |
| Scanlan | | Irish | Devious |
| Scorpio | | Latin | Scorpion. Star sign and constellation |
| Scorpion | | English | Scorpion, arachnid with a poisonous sting |
| Scott | | Anglo-Saxon | From Scotland |
| Seamus | | Irish | He who replaces |
| Sean | Shaun | Irish | God is gracious |
| Sebastian | | Latin | From Bastia in Spain |
| Seff | | Hebrew | A wolf |
| Seif | | Arabic | Sword of religion |
| Selim | | Arabic | Safe |
| Selwin | | Anglo-Saxon | Friend at court |
| Selwyn | | Anglo-Saxon | Friend at court |
| Senon | | Spanish | Ivory treasure |
| Senwe | | African | Dry grain stalk |
| Serafino | | Italian | Shining angel |

| Name | Alternate spellings | Origin | Meaning |
|------|---------------------|--------|---------|
| Serge | | French | Servant |
| Sergei | | Russian | Servant |
| Sergio | | Italian | He who cares for |
| Seth | | Hebrew | The appointed one, one of the sons of Adam in the bible |
| Severo | | Italian | Strict, severe |
| Severus | | Latin | Strict, severe |
| Seville | | Spanish | Place name: Spanish city |
| Seyed | | Arabic | The lord |
| Seymore | | French | From town St Maur |
| Shadow | | English | |
| Shafiq | | Arabic | Compassionate |
| Shaine | | Irish | God is gracious |
| Shakar | | Arabic | Thankful |
| Shakir | | Arabic | Thankful |
| Shamrock | | Anglo-Saxon | Plant, emblem of Ireland |
| Shamus | | Irish | He who replaces |
| Shandy | | Anglo-Saxon | Small and boisterous |
| Shane | | Irish | God is gracious |
| Shankar | | Sanskrit | He who gives happiness |
| Shannon | | Irish | Old river |
| Sharif | | Arabic | The honourable one |
| Sharma | | Sanskrit | Protector |
| Shaun | Sean | Irish | God is gracious |
| Shauny | | Irish | God is gracious |
| Shayne | Shane | Irish | God is gracious |
| Shelby | | Anglo-Saxon | Willow farm |
| Sheldon | | Anglo-Saxon | Farm on the ledge |

| Name | Alternate spellings | Origin | Meaning |
|------|---------------------|--------|---------|
| Shelley | | Anglo-Saxon | Farm on the ledge |
| Sher | | Sanskrit | The beloved one |
| Sherlock | | Literary | *Adventures of Sherlock Holmes* by Sir Arthur Conan Doyle |
| Sherwin | Sherwyn | Anglo-Saxon | Quick as the wind |
| Shiloh | | Hebrew | A place of rest |
| Shipley | | Anglo-Saxon | From the sheep meadow |
| Shiva | | Sanskrit | Benign. A Hindu god |
| Shmon | | Hebrew | The listener |
| Shunnar | | Arabic | Pleasant |
| Siddartha | | Sanskrit | One who has accomplished his goal. A name of the Buddha |
| Sidney | | French | A follower of St Denis |
| Siegfried | | German | Peaceful victory |
| Siegmund | | German | Victorious protector |
| Silas | | Latin | Of the forest |
| Silvano | | Italian | From the forest |
| Silvester | Sylvester | Latin | Of the forest |
| Silvestro | | Italian | From the forest |
| Silvio | | Italian | From the forest |
| Simon | | Hebrew | The listener |
| Sinbad | | Literary | *The Book of 1001 Arabian Nights* |
| Sinclair | | Anglo-Saxon | St Clair |
| Sindri | | Scandinavian | A mythical dwarf |
| Sinjon | | Anglo-Saxon | St John |

| Name | Alternate spellings | Origin | Meaning |
|------|---------------------|--------|---------|
| Sirio | | Italian | The Dog Star |
| Sirius | | Latin | The Dog Star, the brightest in the night sky |
| Skelly | | Scottish | Historian |
| Skip | | Scandinavian | Ship-owner |
| Slade | | Anglo-Saxon | From the valley |
| Slater | | American | From the surname |
| Smith | Smythe | Anglo-Saxon | Blacksmith |
| Smokey | | Anglo-Saxon | Vapour from a fire |
| Sol | | Latin | The sun |
| Solomon | | Hebrew | Wise and peaceful |
| Sondre | | Scandinavian | Uncertain |
| Soren | | Scandinavian | Severe |
| Sorrel | | French | Brown haired |
| Soul | | English | Spirit |
| Sparky | | American | Man about town |
| Sparrow | | English | Small bird |
| Spike | | English | Nickname for someone with spiky hair |
| Spirit | | English | Soul, non-physical being |
| Stacey | | Greek | Resurrection |
| Stanley | | Anglo-Saxon | From the stoney meadow |
| Starr | | Anglo-Saxon | Star |
| Stavros | | Greek | Crowned |
| Stefan | | German | Crown |
| Stefano | | Italian | Crown |
| Stelios | | Greek | Crown |
| Stéphane | | French | Crown |
| Stephen | Steve, Stevie | Greek | Crown |
| Steven | Steve, Stevie | Greek | Crown |

| Name | Alternate spellings | Origin | Meaning |
|------|---------------------|--------|---------|
| Stewart | | Anglo-Saxon | Steward |
| Storm | | Anglo-Saxon | Thunder and lightening |
| Stuart | Stewart | Anglo-Saxon | Steward |
| Sugar Ray | | American | Name of famous boxer, Sugar Ray Leonard |
| Sullivan | | Irish | Dark eyes |
| Suman | | Sanskrit | Cheerful and wise |
| Summit | | English | Peak of a mountain |
| Sumner | | Anglo-Saxon | Summoner |
| Suresh | | Sanskrit | The ruler of the gods |
| Surya | | Sanskrit | The sun |
| Sven | | Scandinavian | Boy |
| Sverre | | Scandinavian | Spinner, turner |
| Sweeney | | Irish | Young hero |
| Sylvester | Silvester | Latin | Of the forest |
| Symon | | Hebrew | The listener |

| Name | Alternate spellings | Origin | Meaning |
|------|---------------------|--------|---------|

## T

| Name | Alternate spellings | Origin | Meaning |
|------|---------------------|--------|---------|
| Tahir | | Arabic | Pure and virtuous |
| Tahir | | African | Pure |
| Taj | | Sanskrit | Royal |
| Taji | | African | Crown |
| Tajo | | Spanish | Day |
| Talbot | | French | Reward |
| Talib | | African | Seeker |
| Taliesin | | Welsh | Shining brow. Legendary Welsh poet |
| Tama | | Pacific Islands | Son |
| Tamir | | Arabic | Pure, tall |
| Tane | | Pacific Islands | A Polynesian god |
| Tangaroa | | Pacific Islands | Of the sea |
| Tariq | | Arabic | The night visitor |
| Tarquin | | Latin | Name of Roman kings |
| Tarun | | Sanskrit | Young, tender |
| Tate | | Anglo-Saxon | Uncertain |
| Taurus | | Latin | The bull. Star sign and constellation |
| Tawhiri | | Pacific Islands | A storm |
| Taylor | | Anglo-Saxon | Cutter, clothes maker |
| Ted | | Anglo-Saxon | From Edward, wealthy guardian |
| Terence | | Latin | Tender, gracious |
| Terenzio | | Italian | Soft, tender |
| Terry | | Latin | Tender, gracious |
| Texas | | Place name | US state |
| Thaddeus | | Greek | Gift of God |
| Thane | | Anglo-Saxon | Protective |

| Name | Alternate spellings | Origin | Meaning |
|------|---------------------|--------|---------|
| Theo | | Greek | God like |
| Theobald | | Anglo-Saxon | Of the brave people |
| Théodore | | French | Gift of God |
| Theodore | | Greek | Gift of God |
| Théophile | | French | Friend of God |
| Theron | | Greek | A wild beast |
| Thierry | | French | Ruler of the people |
| Thomas | | Greek | A twin |
| Tiernan | | Irish | Regal |
| Tiger | | English | Striped predatory 'big' cat |
| Tiki | | Pacific Islands | Spirit fetched from death to return to life |
| Tim | | Greek | Honoured by God |
| Timor | | Place name | Island in Indonesia |
| Timothy | Tim | Greek | Honoured by God |
| Tipple | | American | Slang for a drink |
| Titan | | Greek | Giant |
| Tito | | Italian | Defender |
| Titus | | Greek | Giant |
| Tivon | | Latin | Lover of nature |
| Tobias | Toby | Latin | God is good |
| Tobie | Toby | Latin | God is good |
| Toby | Tobie | Latin | God is good |
| Todd | | Latin | Fox |
| Tom | Thom | Greek | A twin |
| Tomas | | Spanish | Twin |
| Tommaso | | Italian | Twin |
| Tommy | | Greek | A twin |
| Tomo | | Greek | A twin |
| Tony | Toni | Latin | Praiseworthy |

| Name | Alternate spellings | Origin | Meaning |
|------|---------------------|--------|---------|
| Tor | | Anglo-Saxon | Rock formation on moorland peak |
| Tor | Thor | Scandinavian | From the God of Thunder, Thor |
| Torrence | | Latin | Smooth |
| Travis | | Anglo-Saxon | Crossing |
| Trent | | Latin | Quick-minded |
| Trevor | | Irish | Prudent |
| Trey | | American | Three in a suit of playing cards |
| Tristan | Trystan, Tristram | Welsh, Cornish | Sad. A tragic, romantic hero in Celtic legend |
| Tristram | Tristan, Trystan | Welsh | Sad. A tragic, romantic hero in Celtic legend |
| Troy | | Irish | Foot soldier |
| Truman | | Anglo-Saxon | Honest |
| Trystan | Tristan, Tristram | Welsh, Cornish | Sad. A tragic, romantic hero in Celtic legend |
| Tucker | | Anglo-Saxon | Garment maker, 'tucker of cloth' |
| Tuily | | Irish | Interesting |
| Turi | | Pacific Islands | A famous chief |
| Turner | | Latin | Craftsman |
| Tyler | | Anglo-Saxon | A tiler |
| Tyonne | | American | Feisty |
| Tyrol | | | Place name: Region of the Alps |
| Tyrone | | Irish | County in Northern Ireland |
| Tyson | | French | High spirited |

| Name | Alternate spellings | Origin | Meaning |
|---|---|---|---|

## U

| Name | Alternate spellings | Origin | Meaning |
|---|---|---|---|
| Ubora | | African | Excellence |
| Udd | | Hebrew | Praised |
| Ulan | | African | First-born twin |
| Ulrich | | German | Riches, power |
| Ulrik | | Scandinavian | Powerful and wealthy |
| Ulysses | | Greek | Angry one |
| Umar | | Arabic | Long-lived |
| Umar | | African | Longevity |
| Umber | | Anglo-Saxon | Orange, brown colour |
| Umberto | | Italian | Magnificent giant |
| Unique | | English | One of a kind |
| Urban | | Latin | City dweller |
| Uriah | | Hebrew | The light of God |
| Uriel | | Hebrew | The light of God |
| Uriele | | Italian | The light of God |
| Usher | | Latin | Decisive |
| Ushnisha | | Sanskrit | A crown |
| Usman | | Arabic | A servant of God. |
| Utah | | Place name | US state |
| Uther | | Cornish | Legendary king, father of King Arthur |
| Utopia | | Greek | Perfect place |
| Uwan | | Australian | To meet |

| Name | Alternate spellings | Origin | Meaning |
|------|--------------------|--------|---------|

## V

| Name | Alternate spellings | Origin | Meaning |
|------|--------------------|--------|---------|
| Vadim | | Russian | To rule with greatness |
| Valentine | | Latin | Strong, healthy, patron saint of lovers |
| Valentino | | Italian | Strong, healthy, patron saint of lovers |
| Valerio | | Italian | Courageous |
| Vamana | | Sanskrit | Praiseworthy |
| Van | | American | Short for Ivan or Evan |
| Vance | | Anglo-Saxon | Brash |
| Vanya | | Russian | Right |
| Varuna | | Sanskrit | The God of the night sky |
| Vasili | | Russian | King |
| Vassilly | Vassily | Russian | King |
| Vasudeva | | Sanskrit | The father of the God Krishna |
| Vaughn | | Welsh | Small |
| Vegas | | Place name | From US city Las Vegas, the meadows |
| Vere | | Anglo-Saxon | Alder tree |
| Vernon | | Latin | Youthful |
| Vic | | Latin | Conqueror |
| Victor | | Latin | Conqueror |
| Vidal | | Latin | Vital, lively |
| Vidya | | Sanskrit | Knowledge |
| Vijay | | Sanskrit | Strong and victorious |
| Viktor | | Russian | Victory |
| Vimal | | Sanskrit | Pure |
| Vince | | Latin | Conqueror |
| Vincent | | Latin | Conqueror |

| Name | Alternate spellings | Origin | Meaning |
|------|---------------------|--------|---------|
| Vincenzo | | Italian | Conqueror |
| Vinnie | | Latin | Conqueror |
| Virgil | | Latin | Strong |
| Vishnu | | Sanskrit | The protector. A Hindu god |
| Vitale | | Italian | Full of life |
| Vitali | | Russian | Vitality |
| Vito | | Italian | Belligerent |
| Vittore | | Italian | Winner |
| Vittorio | | Spanish | Winner |
| Vitya | | Russian | Vitality |
| Vivian | | French | Vivacious |
| Vlad | | Russian | Ruler |
| Vladislav | | Russian | Glorious rule |
| Vladja | | Russian | Glorious rule |
| Vladmir | | Russian | To rule with greatness |
| Voldemort | | Latin | Flight from death |
| Volker | | German | Prepared to defend |
| Volodya | | Russian | To rule with greatness |
| Volya | | Russian | To rule all |

| Name | Alternate spellings | Origin | Meaning |
|------|---------------------|--------|---------|
| **W** | | | |
| Wahib | | Arabic | The generous one |
| Waitimu | | African | Born of the spear |
| Waldo | | German | Ruler |
| Walid | | Arabic | The newborn boy |
| Wallace | | Anglo-Saxon | From Wales |
| Wallis | | Anglo-Saxon | From Wales |
| Walter | Wally | Anglo-Saxon | Army ruler |
| Warra | | Australian | Water |
| Warren | | Anglo-Saxon | Watchman |
| Warwick | | Place name | UK town |
| Wasim | | Arabic | The handsome one |
| Wassily | | Sanskrit | The God of the night sky |
| Wayne | | Anglo-Saxon | Cart owner |
| Webster | | Anglo-Saxon | Weaver |
| Wendel | | German | Of the Wend people |
| Wilbur | | Anglo-Saxon | Walled fort |
| Wilfred | | Anglo-Saxon | Strong peacemaker |
| Wilhelm | | German | Strong protector |
| Will | | German | Strong protector |
| Willard | | German | Courageous |
| Willis | | Anglo-Saxon | From William, strong protector |
| Wilson | | Anglo-Saxon | Son of William |
| Windsor | | Place name | UK town. Also the Royal family's surname |
| Winston | | Anglo-Saxon | Friendly town. Also after Winston Churchill |

| Name | Alternate spellings | Origin | Meaning |
|------|---------------------|--------|---------|
| Wolf | | German | Wolf |
| Wolfgang | | German | Wolf, going |
| Woodrow | | Anglo-Saxon | From the row of houses by the wood |
| Woody | | Anglo-Saxon | Of the trees |
| Wordsworth | | Anglo-Saxon | Surname of poet, William Wordsworth |
| Worth | | Anglo-Saxon | Enclosure |
| Wycliff | | Anglo-Saxon | By the cliff |
| Wyndham | | Anglo-Saxon | Hamlet near a path |
| Wynne | | Anglo-Saxon | Friend |

| Name | Alternate spellings | Origin | Meaning |
|------|---------------------|--------|---------|

## X

| Name | Alternate spellings | Origin | Meaning |
|------|---------------------|--------|---------|
| Xander | | Greek | Defender of mankind |
| Xanthus | | Greek | Golden haired |
| Xavier | | French, Spanish, Italian | Luminous |
| Xen | | American | From Zen |
| Xeno | | Greek | Stranger |
| Xerxes | | Arabic | Leader |
| Xyle | | American | Helpful |

| Name | Alternate spellings | Origin | Meaning |
|------|--------------------|--------|---------|
| | | | |

## Y

| Name | Alternate spellings | Origin | Meaning |
|------|--------------------|--------|---------|
| Yadon | | American | Surname used as a first name |
| Yakim | | Russian | Established by God |
| Yakov | | Russian | He who replaces |
| Yale | | Welsh | Arable upland |
| Yan | | Hebrew | God's grace |
| Yancy | | American | From Yankee |
| Yanis | | Hebrew | God's grace |
| Yannis | | Greek | Believer |
| Yardley | | Anglo-Saxon | Fenced meadow |
| Yaroslav | | Russian | Spring glory |
| Yarran | | Australian | An acacia tree |
| Yasha | | Russian | He who replaces |
| Yasir | | Arabic | Wealthy |
| Yazid | | Arabic | Ever increasing |
| Yeats | | Literary | Surname of famous Irish poet, W. B. Yeats |
| Yehudi | | Hebrew | Praise to the Lord |
| Yoel | | Hebrew | From Joel, Yaweh is God |
| Yohance | | African | Gift from God |
| Yorick | | Literary | *Hamlet* by William Shakespeare |
| York | | Place name | UK city |
| Yukon | | Place name | From US region meaning great river |
| Yuma | | Place name | City in Arizona, USA |
| Yuri | | Russian | Farmer |
| Yves | | French | Yew |

| Name | Alternate spellings | Origin | Meaning |
|------|---------------------|--------|---------|
| **z** | | | |
| Zaccheus | | Hebrew | Unblemished |
| Zacharie | | French | The Lord has remembered |
| Zachary | | Hebrew | The Lord has remembered |
| Zachria | | Hebrew | The Lord has remembered |
| Zade | | Arabic | Flourishing |
| Zadok | | Hebrew | Unyielding |
| Zafar | | Arabic | The triumphant one |
| Zahir | | Arabic | Shining |
| Zahir | | African | Shining |
| Zaie | | American | Pleasure-seeking |
| Zain | | American | Zany |
| Zaire | | Place name | African country |
| Zakhar | | Russian | God remembers |
| Zaki | | Arabic | Pure |
| Zamir | | Hebrew | A songbird |
| Zander | | Greek | Defender of mankind |
| Zane | | Literary | Name of writer, Zane Grey |
| Zareb | | African | Protector |
| Zavier | | Spanish | Luminous |
| Zebediah | | Hebrew | Gift of god |
| Zed | | Hebrew | Energetic |
| Zekeriah | | Hebrew | The Lord has remembered |
| Zen | | Japanese | Spiritual |
| Zeth | | Greek | Investigator |
| Zeus | | Greek | The supreme god in Greek mythology |
| Zevi | | Hebrew | Brisk |

| Name | Alternate spellings | Origin | Meaning |
|------|---------------------|--------|---------|
| Zia | | Arabic | Splendour or ripened grain |
| Zion | | Hebrew | A sign |
| Zowie | | Celebrity child | (David and Iman Bowie) |
| Zuri | | African | Handsome |

# 05

## girls' names
## a to z

**In this chapter you will learn:**
- the origin of your favourite names
- the meaning of your favourite names
- alternative spellings and names that sound similar.

| Name | Alternate spellings | Origin | Meaning |
|------|---------------------|--------|---------|
| **A** | | | |
| Aaliyah | | Arabic | Exalted |
| Aba | | African | Born on Thursday |
| Abayomi | | African | Come to bring joy |
| Abbie | Abby, Abbey | Hebrew | Father's joy |
| Abebi | | African | Asked for |
| Abela | | Italian | |
| Abelia | | Hebrew | Breath |
| Abelina | | Italian | |
| Abeo | | African | Bringer of happiness |
| Abia | | Arabic | Great |
| Abigail | Abby, Abi, Abbie | Hebrew | Father's joy |
| Abir | | Arabic | Fragrant |
| Abla | | African | Wild rose |
| Acacia | | | A flower/tree |
| Acorn | | Anglo-Saxon | The seed of an oak tree |
| Ada | | German | Noble |
| Adaeze | | African | Princess |
| Adah | | Hebrew | Adornment or ornament |
| Adalberta | | German | Noble, famous |
| Adalgisa | | German | Noble promise |
| Adalia | | Hebrew | God is my refuge |
| Adan | | Irish | Little fiery one |
| Adande | | African | Challenger |
| Adanma | | African | Daughter of beauty |
| Adanna | | African | Father's daughter |
| Adanne | | African | Mother's daughter |

| Name | Alternate spellings | Origin | Meaning |
|------|---------------------|--------|---------|
| Adar | | Arabic | Fire |
| Adara | Adhara | Arabic | Virgin. Name of a star |
| Addolorata | | Italian | Sorrows |
| Adelaide | | Italian | Noble |
| Adèle | | French | Noble |
| Adelfina | | Italian | Sisterly |
| Adelheide | | German | Noble |
| Adelia | | Italian | Noble |
| Adelinda | | Italian | Noble |
| Adelpha | | Greek | Sisterly |
| Adena | | Hebrew | Delicate, slender |
| Adero | | African | Life giver |
| Adiba | | Arabic | Cultured |
| Adila | | Arabic | Equal |
| Adiva | | Arabic | Pleasant, gentle |
| Adjua | | African | Born on Monday |
| Adoncia | | Spanish | Owner |
| Adriana | | Latin | From Hadria, Northern Italy |
| Adrienne | | French | From Hadria, Northern Italy |
| Adwin | | African | Artist |
| Adzo | | African | Born on Monday |
| Aerien | | French | Airy |
| Afam | | African | Friendly |
| Afi | | African | Born on Friday |
| Afraima | | Arabic | Fruitful |
| Africa | | Place name | A continent |
| Agafaya | | Russian | Love |
| Agape | | Greek | Love |
| Agatha | | Greek | Kind, honourable |
| Agathe | | French | Kind, honourable |
| Agbeko | | African | Life |
| Aglaya | | Russian | Beauty |

| Name | Alternate spellings | Origin | Meaning |
|------|---------------------|--------|---------|
| Agnes | | Greek | Pure, chaste |
| Agnessa | | Russian | Chaste |
| Aidan | | Irish | Little fiery one |
| Aidoo | | African | Arrived |
| Aiesha | | Arabic | Woman |
| Aileen | | Scottish | Light bearer |
| Ailsa | | Scottish | Island dweller |
| Aimée | | French | Loved |
| Ain | | Arabic | Precious |
| Aine | | Irish | Grace |
| Aiofe | | Irish | Beauty |
| Aisha | | Arabic | Life |
| Aislin | | Irish | Dream, vision |
| Aithne | | Irish | Fire |
| Akala | | Australian | A parrot |
| Akila | | Arabic | Wise |
| Akilah | | Arabic | Intelligent |
| Akili | | African | Wisdom |
| Akilina | | Russian | Eagle |
| Aksinya | | Russian | Hospitality |
| Akuabia | | African | Here is wealth |
| Akuako | | African | Younger twin |
| Akwate | | African | Older twin |
| Alaba | | African | Second baby |
| Alaezi | | African | Exonerated |
| Alana | Alannah | Irish | Attractive |
| Alanis | Alannis | Greek | From Atlanta, mythical city beneath the sea |
| Alannah | Alana | Irish | Attractive |
| Alatea | | Spanish | Truth |
| Alayna | | Irish | Attractive |
| Alberta | | German | Noble and bright |
| Albertina | | Italian | Noble and bright |
| Albina | | Italian | White |
| Alda | | Italian | Beautiful |

| Name | Alternate spellings | Origin | Meaning |
| --- | --- | --- | --- |
| Aldonza | | Spanish | Sweet |
| Alea | | French | Chance |
| Aleida | | German | Noble |
| Alejandra | | Spanish | Defender of mankind |
| Aleksandra | | Russian | Defender of mankind |
| Aleksandrina | | Russian | Defender of mankind |
| Alessandra | | Greek | Defender of man |
| Alessandria | | Greek | Defender of man |
| Alethea | | Greek | Truth |
| Alex | | Greek | Defender of man |
| Alexandra | | Greek | Defender of man |
| Alexis | | Greek | Defender of mankind |
| Alfonsina | | Italian | Noble and brave |
| Alfreda | | Italian | Counsellor of the elves |
| Alfredina | | Italian | Counsellor of the elves |
| Ali | | Arabic | Exalted |
| Alice | | Greek | Wise, truthful one |
| Alicia | Alisha | Greek | Wise, truthful one |
| Alida | | Latin | Small and winged |
| Alima | | Arabic | Musician, dancer |
| Alinga | | Australian | The sun |
| Alison | Allie | Greek | Wise, truthful one |
| Alita | Alida | Spanish | Small winged one |
| Aliya | | Arabic | Sublime, exalted |
| Aliyah | | Arabic | Exalted |
| Alize | | French | Soft cloud |
| Alkina | | Australian | The moon |

| Name | Alternate spellings | Origin | Meaning |
|------|---------------------|--------|---------|
| Alkira | | Australian | The sky |
| Allegra | | Italian | Joyful |
| Allegra | | Spanish | Joyful, lively |
| Alma | | Hebrew | Of the soul |
| Almira | | Arabic | Truth without question |
| Aloisia | | Italian | In the light |
| Alvira | Elvira | Spanish | Foreign, stranger |
| Alvisa | | Italian | Wise one of the household |
| Alyetoro | | African | Peace on Earth |
| Alyona | | Russian | Moon |
| Alyssa | | Greek | Wise, truthful one |
| Alzena | | Arabic | A woman |
| Ama | | African | Born on Saturday |
| Amala | | Arabic | Hope |
| Amalia | | Italian | Energetic |
| Amalie | | French | Hard working |
| Amana | | Hebrew | Faithful or loyal |
| Amanda | | Hebrew | Worthy of being loved |
| Amani | | Arabic | Desire |
| Amara | | Greek | Eternal beauty |
| Amarante | | French | Flower |
| Amarina | | Australian | Rain |
| Amaryllis | | Greek | Shepherdess |
| Amata | | Spanish | Beloved |
| Ambar | | Sanskrit | Of the sky |
| Amber | | Arabic | Golden orange gemstone |
| Ambra | | Arabic | Golden orange gemstone |
| Ambretta | | Italian | Golden orange gemstone |
| Ameerah | | Arabic | Princess |

| Name | Alternate spellings | Origin | Meaning |
|------|---------------------|--------|---------|
| Amélie | | French | Hard working, industrious |
| Amerique | | French | America |
| Amina | | Arabic | Honest, faithful |
| Aminta | | Greek | Protector |
| Amira | | Arabic | A princess |
| Amity | | Latin | Friendship |
| Amrita | | Sanskrit | Immortal |
| Anabelle | | Latin | Loveable |
| Anaïs | | French | Grace |
| Anan | | Arabic | Of the clouds |
| Ananda | | Sanskrit | Joyful |
| Anastasia | | Russian | Resurrection |
| Anastasie | | French | She who will rise again |
| Andrea | | Greek | Strong |
| Andrée | | French | Strong |
| Andy | | Greek | Strong |
| Ange | | French | Angel |
| Angel | | English | Heavenly messenger |
| Angela | | Greek | Heavenly messenger |
| Angelica | | Greek | Heavenly messenger |
| Angelina | | Italian | Angel |
| Angelou | | Spanish | Angel |
| Anila | | Sanskrit | Of the wind |
| Anisa | | Arabic | Friendly |
| Anita | | Italian | Grace |
| Anjanette | | French | Blend of Anne and Janet, gift of God's grace |
| Anna | | Italian | Grace |
| Anna Maria | | Italian | Grace, bitter |
| Annabel | | Italian | Grace, beauty |
| Annabella | | Italian | Grace, beauty |
| Anne | | Hebrew | Grace |

| Name | Alternate spellings | Origin | Meaning |
|------|--------------------|--------|---------|
| Annika | | Scandinavian | Gracious |
| Annisa | | American | Blend of Anne and Lisa |
| Annissa | | Arabic | Charming, gracious |
| Anouk | | French | Grace |
| Anouska | | Russian | Grace |
| Anthea | | Hebrew | Flower like |
| Antoinette | | French | Praiseworthy |
| Antonella | | Italian | Worthy of praise |
| Antonia | | Latin | Praiseworthy |
| Antonietta | | Italian | Worthy of praise |
| Antonina | | Russian | Praiseworthy |
| Anushka | | Russian | Grace |
| Apanie | | Australian | Water |
| Aphrodite | | Greek | Goddess of beauty and love |
| Apple | | Anglo-Saxon | A fruit |
| Apple | | Celebrity child | (Gwyneth Paltrow and Chris Martin) |
| April | | Latin | From first Roman month, start of spring |
| Aquarius | | Latin | Water bearer. Star sign and constellation |
| Arabella | | Latin | Beautiful altar |
| Araluen | | Australian | The place of water lilies |
| Araminta | | Greek | Fragrant flower |
| Aretha | | Greek | The best |
| Aria | | Latin | Beautiful melody |
| Ariana | Arianna | Latin | Most holy |
| Arianwyn | | Welsh | Silver and fair, blessed |
| Arika | | Australian | A water lily |

| Name | Alternate spellings | Origin | Meaning |
|------|---------------------|--------|---------|
| Arina | | Russian | Peace |
| Arinya | | Australian | A kangaroo |
| Arlene | | American | Promise |
| Arlene | | Scottish | Pledge |
| Arlinda | | American | Blend of Arleen (promise) and Linda (pretty) |
| Artemisia | | Italian | From Artemis, Goddess of the moon and hunting |
| Aruna | | Sanskrit | The dawn |
| Arwen | | Literary | *Lord of the Rings* by J. R. R. Tolkein |
| Arwyn | | Welsh | Muse |
| Asa | | Scandinavian | Divine |
| Ash | | Anglo-Saxon | A tree |
| Asha | | Sanskrit | Hope |
| Asha | | African | Life |
| Ashira | | Hebrew | Wealthy |
| Ashley | Ashleigh | Anglo-Saxon | From the meadow of ash trees |
| Asia | | Greek | East |
| Asta | | Greek | A star |
| Astra | | Greek | Like a star |
| Astrid | | Scandinavian | Divine, beautiful |
| Asya | | Russian | Resurrection |
| Athena | | Greek | Goddess of wisdom and war |
| Atifa | | Arabic | Affection |
| Atiya | | Arabic | A gift |
| Atlanta | | Place name | US city. From the mythical city beneath the waves |
| Audrey | | Anglo-Saxon | Of noble strength |

| Name | Alternate spellings | Origin | Meaning |
|------|--------------------|--------|---------|
| Aura | | Greek | Of the air |
| Aurelia | | Latin | Golden |
| Aurélie | | French | Golden |
| Auretta | | Italian | Gentle breeze |
| Auriga | | Latin | Charioteer. A constellation |
| Aurora | | Italian | Dawn, Roman Goddess of the morning |
| Aurore | | French | Dawn |
| Autumn | | Anglo-Saxon | The season before winter |
| Ava | | Greek | An eagle |
| Avalon | | Celtic | An island paradise in Celtic mythology |
| Avara | | Sanskrit | The youngest |
| Avril | | French | April |
| Ayanna | | African | Beautiful flower |
| Ayn | | Russian | Grace |
| Azalea | | Greek | A flower |
| Aziza | | Arabic | Cherished one |
| Azra | | Arabic | Virginal |
| Azure | | English | Blue, green |

| Name | Alternate spellings | Origin | Meaning |
| --- | --- | --- | --- |
| **B** | | | |
| Baako | | African | First born |
| Baba | | African | Born on Thursday |
| Babe | | American | Slang for cute girl |
| Babette | | French | Stranger |
| Badu | | African | Tenth child |
| Bahati | | African | Lucky |
| Bailey | | French | Bailiff |
| Bakana | | Australian | A watcher |
| Bala | | Sanskrit | A young girl |
| Barakah | | Arabic | Fair one |
| Barbara | | Latin | Stranger |
| Barbro | | Scandinavian | Stranger |
| Barina | | Australian | The summit |
| Basimah | | Arabic | The smiling one |
| Bathilda | | Hebrew | Heroine |
| Bathsheba | | Hebrew | Daughter of the oath |
| Batilda | | Italian | Battler |
| Beatrice | | Latin | Blessed, voyager through life |
| Beatrix | | Anglo-Saxon | Bringer of happiness |
| Bega | | Australian | Beautiful |
| Begonia | | Latin | A flower |
| Belicia | | Spanish | Pet name of Isabel, God's promise |
| Belinda | | Italian | Beautiful, tender |
| Belita | | Spanish | Little beauty |
| Bella | | French | Beautiful |
| Bellatrix | | Latin | Female warrior |
| Belle | | French | Beautiful |
| Belphoebe | | Literary | *The Fairie Queen* by Edmund Spenser |

| Name | Alternate spellings | Origin | Meaning |
|------|---------------------|--------|---------|
| Benada | | African | Born on Tuesday |
| Benedicta | | Latin | Blessed |
| Bennath | | Cornish | Blessing |
| Berenice | | Greek | Bringer of victory |
| Bernadette | | French | Brave as a bear |
| Berry | | Anglo-Saxon | Like a fruit |
| Berta | | German | Bright, famous |
| Bertha | | German | Bright, famous |
| Beryl | | Greek | Precious green gem |
| Beth | | Hebrew | My God is a vow |
| Bethany | | Hebrew | House of figs |
| Betty | | Hebrew | Short for Elizabeth, God is my vow |
| Beyonce | | American | From the Creole surname Beyince |
| Bianca | | Italian | White |
| Bibi | | Arabic | A lady |
| Bibiana | | Italian | Lively |
| Bijou | | French | Jewel |
| Billie | | Anglo-Saxon | Strong protector |
| Binah | | African | Dancer |
| Binda | | Australian | Deep water |
| Binta | | African | With God |
| Birgit | | Scandinavian | Exalted one |
| Bisa | | African | Loved |
| Blaine | | Irish | Slender |
| Blejan | | Cornish | Bloom |
| Bliss | | English | Happiness |
| Blodeyn | | Welsh | Flower |
| Blodwedd | | Welsh | In Celtic legend, a bride of flowers |
| Blossom | | Anglo-Saxon | Flowers on fruit trees |

| Name | Alternate spellings | Origin | Meaning |
|------|---------------------|--------|---------|
| Bluebell | | Anglo-Saxon | A blue woodland flower |
| Blythe | | Anglo-Saxon | Cheerful |
| Bo | | Scandinavian | Dweller |
| Bobby | | Anglo-Saxon | Bright fame |
| Bogdana | | Russian | Gift from God |
| Bonita | | Spanish | Pretty |
| Bonnie | | Anglo-Saxon | Pretty |
| Bonte | | French | Bounty |
| Borra | | Cornish | Dawn |
| Bracha | | Hebrew | A blessing |
| Bramble | | Anglo-Saxon | Prickly plant |
| Brangwen | Branwen | Welsh | Fair, blessed |
| Breeze | | English | A light wind |
| Bridget | | Irish | The exalted one. Celtic goddess of light and poetry |
| Brie | Bree | French | Marshland |
| Brier | | French | Heather |
| Brighid | | Irish | The exalted one. Celtic goddess of light and poetry |
| Brigid | | Irish | The exalted one. Celtic goddess of light and poetry |
| Brigida | | Italian | Exalted one |
| Brigitte | | French | The exalted one |
| Britt | | Scandinavian | Exalted one |
| Brittany | | Latin | From Britain |
| Bronagh | | Welsh | Sorrowful |
| Bronnen | | Cornish | A rush |
| Brontë | | Literary | From the surname of authors Emily and Charlotte Brontë |

| Name | Alternate spellings | Origin | Meaning |
|------|--------------------|--------|---------|
| Bronwen | | Welsh | Fair, blessed |
| Bronze | | English | Precious metal |
| Brook | Brooke | Anglo-Saxon | A small stream |
| Bruna | | Italian | Brown |
| Bryluen | | Cornish | Rose |
| Bryn | | Welsh | A hill |
| Bryony | | Greek | A vine |
| Buena | | Spanish | Good one |
| Bunme | | African | My gift |

| Name | Alternate spellings | Origin | Meaning |
|------|--------------------|--------|---------|
| **C** | | | |
| Cairo | | Place name | Capital of Egypt |
| Caitlin | | Irish | Pure |
| Cal | | Welsh | Dove |
| Cala | | Arabic | Fortress |
| Calico | | American | Cotton fabric |
| Calla | | Greek | Beautiful |
| Callidora | | Greek | Beautiful gift |
| Callista | | Greek | Most beautiful one |
| Calypso | | Greek | Mythical nymph who fell in love |
| Camden | | Place name | Area in North London |
| Camelia | | Latin | A flower |
| Camilla | | Latin | Noble |
| Camille | | Latin | Virginal, unblemished |
| Camira | | Australian | Of the wind |
| Candice | Candace, Candy | Latin | Brilliance, clarity |
| Candida | | Italian | Bright white |
| Cantara | | Arabic | Bridge |
| Caoimhe | | Irish | Gentle, beauty, grace |
| Capri | | Place name | Italian island |
| Capucine | | French | Cowl |
| Caresse | | French | Beloved |
| Carezza | | Italian | Caress |
| Carina | Karina | Latin | Ship's keel. A constellation |
| Carissa | | Latin | Most beloved one |
| Carla | | Italian | Strong |
| Carlotta | | Italian | Free |

| Name | Alternate spellings | Origin | Meaning |
|------|--------------------|--------|---------|
| Carmel | | Hebrew | Garden, orchard |
| Carmel | | Latin | A garden or orchard |
| Carmela | | Italian | Divine garden |
| Carmelita | | Spanish | Divine garden |
| Carmen | | Spanish | Garden |
| Carmilla | | Hebrew | Garden, orchard |
| Carnation | | English | Flower |
| Carola | | Italian | Strong |
| Carole | | Anglo-Saxon | Strong |
| Carolina | | Italian | Strong |
| Carolyn | | English | Womanly |
| Caron | | French | Pure |
| Caron | | Welsh | To love |
| Carroll | | Literary | From the author, Lewis Carroll |
| Carwyn | | Welsh | Blessed, fair love |
| Cary | | Welsh | Descendant of the dark ones |
| Carys | | Welsh | Love |
| Casey | | Irish | Brave |
| Cassandra | | Greek | Trojan princess who could forsee disaster |
| Cassia | | Latin | From the Cassia (cinnamon) tree |
| Catalina | | Spanish | Pure |
| Catena | | Italian | Pure |
| Caterina | | Italian | Pure |
| Catherine | | Greek | Pure |
| Cayla | | American | From Celtic name Kayleigh (slender) |
| Cécile | | French | Blind one |
| Cecilia | | Latin | Blind one |
| Celena | | Greek | Goddess of the moon |
| Celene | | Greek | Goddess of the moon |

| Name | Alternate spellings | Origin | Meaning |
|------|---------------------|--------|---------|
| Celeste | | Latin | Heavenly |
| Celina | | Greek | Goddess of the moon |
| Celine | | Greek | Goddess of the moon |
| Celyn | | Welsh | Holly |
| Ceri | | Welsh | Blessed, fair poet, goddess of poetic inspiration |
| Ceridwen | | Welsh | Blessed, fair poet, goddess of poetic inspiration |
| Cerise | | | Dark, bright pink |
| Cerulean | | English | A shade of deep blue |
| Cerys | | Welsh | Love |
| Cesarina | | Italian | Hairy |
| Cézanne | | French | Surname of artist, Paul Cézanne |
| Chai | | Hebrew | Life giving |
| Chanah | | Hebrew | Grace |
| Chandani | | Sanskrit | The goddess Devi |
| Chandi | | Sanskrit | Name of goddess Sakti |
| Chandra | | Sanskrit | Bright moon |
| Chanel | Chanelle | French | Pipe, channel. Name of French designer, Coco Chanel |
| Chantal | | French | Song |
| Chante | | French | To sing |
| Charis | | Greek | Grace, charm |
| Charisma | | Greek | Charm and grace |

| Name | Alternate spellings | Origin | Meaning |
|------|---------------------|--------|---------|
| Charissa | | Greek | Grace, charm |
| Charity | | Latin | Loving and generous |
| Charlene | | French | Small beauty |
| Charlize | | French | Free |
| Charlotte | | French | Small and pretty |
| Charmaine | | Latin | Charming |
| Chartreuse | | French | A French liqueur, a shade of green |
| Chastity | | Latin | Pure and chaste |
| Chaton | | French | Kitten |
| Chaya | | Hebrew | Life |
| Chelsea | | Anglo-Saxon | Landing place |
| Cherry | | English | Fruit |
| Cheryl | | French | Dear |
| Chiara | | Italian | Clear, illustrious |
| Chiku | | African | Talkative |
| China | | Place name | Country |
| Chinue | | African | Blessing |
| Chiquita | | Spanish | Little one |
| Chloe | | Greek | Fertile young woman |
| Cho | | Chinese | Beautiful |
| Chocolate | | English | Food and colour |
| Chorus | | English | Refrain in a song, or a choir of voices |
| Chris | | Latin | Follower of Christ |
| Christa | | German | Follower of Christ |
| Christelle | | French | Follower of Christ |
| Christer | | Scandinavian | Follower of Christ |
| Christiane | | French | Follower of Christ |
| Christina | | Latin | Follower of Christ |

| Name | Alternate spellings | Origin | Meaning |
|------|---------------------|--------|---------|
| Christine | | French | Follower of Christ |
| Chrysilla | | Greek | Golden haired |
| Ciara | | Italian | Clear, illustrious |
| Ciara | | Welsh | Little dark one |
| Cilla | | Greek | Short for Lucilla |
| Cindy | | Greek | Short for Lucinda |
| Cinzia | | Italian | Moon |
| Circe | | Greek | Witch in Greek mythology |
| Cirilla | | Italian | Queen |
| Cirrus | | Anglo-Saxon | A form of cloud |
| Claire | Clare | Latin | Clear, illustrious |
| Clara | | Italian | Clear, shining |
| Clarice | | Latin | Little brilliant one |
| Clarissa | | Latin | Intelligent, clear thinking |
| Claudette | | French | Lame one |
| Claudia | | Latin | Lame one |
| Claudine | | French | Lame one |
| Clémence | | French | Compassionate |
| Cleo | | Greek | Glorious one |
| Clio | | Greek | Glorious one |
| Cloud | | Anglo-Saxon | Water vapour in the sky |
| Clover | | Anglo-Saxon | Clover |
| Cochiti | | Spanish | Forgotten |
| Coco | | Spanish | From the cocoa plant, ingredient of chocolate |
| Cody | | American | Helpful |
| Colette | | French | Victory of the people |
| Colleen | | Irish | Young girl |
| Connie | | Latin | Short for Constance |

| Name | Alternate spellings | Origin | Meaning |
|------|---------------------|--------|---------|
| Consuelo | | Spanish | Consolation |
| Cookie | | American | Cute |
| Coorah | | Australian | Woman |
| Cora | | American | Judgement |
| Cora | | Greek | Maiden |
| Coral | | Latin | From the sea |
| Corazon | | Spanish | Heart |
| Coretta | | Literary | Pet name for Cora, invented for *Last of the Mohicans* by James Fenimore Cooper |
| Corey | | Irish | Ravine |
| Corinna | | Italian | Young girl |
| Corinne | | French | Young girl |
| Cornelia | | Latin | A horn |
| Coro | | Italian | Chorus |
| Cortesia | | Spanish | Hill |
| Cosima | | Greek | Perfect harmony |
| Courtney | | French | Courteous |
| Crimson | | English | A shade of red |
| Crisanta | | Latin | From the flower Chrysanthemum |
| Crispina | | Italian | Curly haired |
| Cristiano | | Italian | Follower of Christ |
| Cristina | | Italian | Follower of Christ |
| Crystal | | Anglo-Saxon | Beautiful rock form |
| Crystal | | Greek | Clear as ice |
| Crystin | | Welsh | Christian |
| Cyan | | English | Pale blue |
| Cybill | Cybil, Sybill | Latin | Prophet |
| Cygnus | | Latin | Swan, a constellation |
| Cynthia | | Greek | Moon goddess |

| Name | Alternate spellings | Origin | Meaning |
| --- | --- | --- | --- |
| **D** | | | |
| Dagmar | | Scandinavian | Dear, peaceful girl |
| Dagna | Dag, Dagne | Scandinavian | New day |
| Dahlia | | Latin | A flower |
| Daisy | | Anglo-Saxon | Eye of the day |
| Dakota | | American | American place name, Native American Tribe |
| Dalia | Dahlia | Italian | After the flower Dahlia |
| Dalila | | Italian | From Delilah, poor |
| Damara | | Greek | Gentle girl |
| Damask | | English | Grey, pink |
| Damiana | | Italian | Tamer |
| Damisi | | African | Happy |
| Dana | | Irish | God is my judge |
| Dandelion | | Anglo-Saxon | A bright yellow flower |
| Daniela | | Italian | God is my judge |
| Danielle | | French | God is my judge |
| Dante | | Latin | Enduring. Name of poet Dante Alighieri, author of *The Divine Comedy* |
| Danza | | Italian | Dancer |
| Daphne | | Greek | Nymph who turned into a laurel tree |
| Dara | | Hebrew | Compassionate |
| Darcy | | Anglo-Saxon | Valley town |
| Daria | | Greek | Wealthy |
| Darlene | | French | Darling |
| Darri | | Australian | A track |
| Davina | | Hebrew | The beloved one |

| Name | Alternate spellings | Origin | Meaning |
|------|------|------|------|
| Dawn | | Anglo-Saxon | Daybreak |
| Daya | | Hebrew | Bird |
| Dayla | | Anglo-Saxon | Valley |
| Daytona | | Place name | US city |
| Deandra | | American | Blend of Deirdre and Alexandra |
| Deborah | | Hebrew | The bee (worker) |
| Deianeira | | Greek | Wife of Hercules |
| Deirdre | | Irish | Tragic Irish heroine |
| Deja | | French | Before |
| Delfina | | Italian | Dolphin |
| Delia | | Greek | Name for Goddess of the moon and hunting |
| Delice | | French | Delight |
| Delilah | | Hebrew | Beautiful temptress |
| Delinda | | Italian | Annointed |
| Dell | | Greek | Kind |
| Della | Adela | German | Noble |
| Dellen | | Cornish | Petal |
| Delma | | Spanish | Beauty, eternal goodness |
| Delores | | Spanish | Sorrowful |
| Delphine | | Latin | Woman fom Delphi, or from the flower, delphinium |
| Delphinium | | Latin | A tall flower |
| Delwyn | | Welsh | Pretty, blessed |
| Demelza | | Cornish | Cornish place name. Heroine of Winston Graham's *Poldark* novels |

| Name | Alternate spellings | Origin | Meaning |
|------|---------------------|--------|---------|
| Demetria | | Italian | From Demeter Greek goddess of agriculture |
| Demi | | Latin | Half |
| Deneb | | Arabic | Tail. Name of a star |
| Denise | | Greek | Wine lover |
| Dervla | | Irish | Daughter of Ireland |
| Desiree | | French | Desire |
| Destiny | | English | Fate |
| Devika | | Sanskrit | A little goddess |
| Devon | Devona | Place name | English county |
| Dewi | | American | Fresh |
| Dharma | | Sanskrit | Morality |
| Diamanta | | French | Like diamonds |
| Diana | | Latin | Divine. Goddess of hunting and the moon |
| Diane | Dian | French | Divine |
| Dido | | Greek | Name of a queen |
| Dietlind | | German | Tender people |
| Dilwen | | Welsh | True, genuine and blessed |
| Dilys | | Welsh | Genuine, steadfast |
| Dina | | Italian | Judgement |
| Dinah | | Latin | Judgement |
| Dione | Dionne | Greek | Wine lover |
| Dior | | French | From fashion designer, Christian Dior |
| Disa | | Scandinavian | Divine |
| Diva | | English | Renowned singer |
| Divine | | English | God like |
| Doherty | | Irish | Obstructive |

| Name | Alternate spellings | Origin | Meaning |
|------|---------------------|--------|---------|
| Doli | | African | Doll |
| Dolly | | American | Doll |
| Dolores | | Spanish | Lady of sorrows |
| Domenica | | Italian | Belongs to God |
| Dominga | | Spanish | Belongs to God |
| Dominique | | French | Belongs to God |
| Donatella | | Italian | Donated to God |
| Dora | | Greek | A gift |
| Dore | | French | Golden |
| Doreen | | French | Golden |
| Dori | | French | Golden |
| Dorian | | Greek | Happy |
| Doris | | Greek | Greek goddess of the sea |
| Dorota | | Spanish | God's gift |
| Dorotea | | Italian | God's gift |
| Dorothée | | French | Gift of God |
| Dorothy | | Greek | Gift of God |
| Dove | | English | Bird, symbol of peace |
| Dream | | English | Vision |
| Drew | | Greek | Strong |
| Drina | | Spanish | From Hadria |
| Drusilla | | Latin | Strong |
| Duena | | Spanish | Protect the companion |
| Dulcie | | Latin | Sweet |
| Dulcinea | | Literary | *Don Quixote* by Miguel de Cervantes |
| Duna | | Italian | Sand dune |
| Durga | | Sanskrit | Unattainable. A Hindu goddess |
| Dusk | | Anglo-Saxon | End of the day |
| Dusty | | American | Name of singer, Dusty Springfield |

| Name | Alternate spellings | Origin | Meaning |
|------|---------------------|--------|---------|
| **E** | | | |
| Eartha | | Anglo-Saxon | Earthy |
| Ebba | | German | Boar |
| Ebony | | Greek | Black wood |
| Ebrel | | Cornish | April |
| Echo | | Greek | Name of a nymph Greek mythology |
| Ecstasy | | English | Bliss |
| Edda | | German | Uncertain |
| Eden | | Hebrew | Pleasure |
| Eden | | Hebrew | Place of pleasure |
| Edith | | Anglo-Saxon | Prosperous in war |
| Edna | | Hebrew | Pleasure |
| Edwina | | Anglo-Saxon | Prosperous friend |
| Effie | | Greek | Virtuous |
| Efia | | African | Born on Friday |
| Egypt | | Place name | African country |
| Eileen | | Irish | Light bearer |
| Eira | | Welsh | Snow |
| Ekala | | Australian | A lake |
| Elaine | | Greek | Light of the sun |
| Elda | | Italian | Gift of the sun |
| Eldora | | Spanish | Gift of the sun |
| Eleanor | | Greek | Light of the sun |
| Electra | Elektra | Greek | Brilliant, shining |
| Elegy | | American | Tribute |
| Elena | | Italian | Light of the sun |
| Eleonora | | Italian | Light of the sun |
| Eletta | | Italian | Elite |
| Eliana | | Italian | Yaweh is my God |
| Elisa | | Italian | Yaweh is my God |

| Name | Alternate spellings | Origin | Meaning |
|------|---------------------|--------|---------|
| Elisabetta | | Italian | God is my vow |
| Élise | | French | God is my vow |
| Elisha | | Hebrew | God is my salvation |
| Elissa | | Hebrew | Consecrated to God |
| Elizabeth | | Hebrew | Consecrated to God |
| Elke | | German | Noble |
| Ella | | Italian | Light of the sun |
| Elle | | French | Woman |
| Ellie | | Greek | Light of the sun |
| Ellin | | Australian | To move |
| Elma | | Arabic | Sweet |
| Elodie | | French | Wealthy |
| Élodie | | French | Wealthy stranger |
| Eloise | | French | Intelligent |
| Elsa | | German | God is my vow |
| Else | | Hebrew | Consecrated to God |
| Elspeth | | Scottish | God is my oath |
| Elvia | | Italian | Elfin |
| Elvina | | Anglo-Saxon | Elfin |
| Elvira | | Spanish | Truly foreign |
| Elwyn | | Anglo-Saxon | Elf/wise friend |
| Elysia | | Greek | From the blessed isles |
| Ema | | Pacific Islands | Beloved |
| Emanuela | | Italian | God is with us |
| Emanuela | | Hebrew | God is with us |
| Ember | | American | Variation of Amber |
| Emerald | | Anglo-Saxon | Precious green gem |
| Emil | | German | Rival |
| Emilia | | Italian | Rival |
| Émilie | | French | Rival |

| Name | Alternate spellings | Origin | Meaning |
|------|---------------------|--------|---------|
| Emily | | German | Poised |
| Emma | | German | Whole, universal |
| Emmanuel | | Hebrew | God is with us |
| Emmanuella | | Hebrew | God is with us |
| Emmanuelle | | French | God is with us |
| Emmeline | | German | Work |
| Ena | | Irish | Fire |
| Engracia | | Spanish | Graceful |
| Enid | | Welsh | Lively |
| Enor | | Cornish | Honour |
| Enrica | | Italian, Spanish | Ruler of the home |
| Eowyn | | Literary | *Lord of the Rings* by J. R. R. Tolkein |
| Eponin | | Literary | *Les Miserables* by Victor Hugo |
| Erika | | Scandinavian | Honourable |
| Erin | | Irish | From Ireland |
| Erma | | Latin | Wealthy |
| Ermentrude | | German | Whole, strong |
| Ernestina | | Italian | Brave like an eagle |
| Eshe | | African | Life |
| Esmeralda | | Spanish | Emerald |
| Esperanza | | Spanish | Hope |
| Estelle | | Latin | A star |
| Ester | | Spanish | Like a star |
| Esther | | Arabic | A star |
| Etenia | | American | Native American word for riches |
| Ethel | | Anglo-Saxon | Noble |
| Etta | | Anglo-Saxon | From Henrietta, ruler of the home |
| Eudora | | Greek | Good gift |
| Eunice | | Greek | Victorious |

| Name | Alternate spellings | Origin | Meaning |
| --- | --- | --- | --- |
| Euphoria | | English | Extreme happiness |
| Eustacia | | Greek | Fruitful |
| Eva | | Italian | Life giving |
| Evangelia | | Greek | One who brings good news |
| Eve | | Hebrew | Life giving |
| Evelyn | | Hebrew | Life giving |
| Ezra | | Hebrew | Happy |

| Name | Alternate spellings | Origin | Meaning |
|------|--------------------|--------|---------|

# F

| Name | Alternate spellings | Origin | Meaning |
|------|--------------------|--------|---------|
| Fabiana | | Italian | Bean grower |
| Fabiola | | Italian | Bean grower |
| Fabrizia | | Italian | Craftsman |
| Fadhila | | African | Outstanding |
| Fadila | | Arabic | Generous and distinguished |
| Faith | | English | |
| Faiza | | Arabic | Victorious |
| Farah | | Arabic | Happiness |
| Farida | | Arabic | Unique |
| Fatima | | Arabic | Daughter of the prophet Mohamed |
| Fatin | | Arabic | Captivating |
| Fausta | | Italian | Lucky |
| Fawn | | English | Young deer |
| Fay | Faye | Anglo-Saxon | Fairy |
| Federica | | Italian | Brave peacemaker |
| Fedora | | Russian | Gift of God |
| Fedra | | Italian | Brave peacemaker |
| Felicia | | Latin | Happy |
| Felicita | | Italian | Lucky one |
| Felicity | | Latin | Lucky, fortunate |
| Felipa | | Spanish | Lover of horses |
| Felita | | Latin | Happy |
| Fen | | Anglo-Saxon | Flat coastal plain |
| Ferdinanda | | Italian | Brave peacemaker |
| Fern | | Anglo-Saxon | A plant |
| Ffion | | Welsh | Fair |
| Fiamma | | Italian | Flame |

| Name | Alternate spellings | Origin | Meaning |
|------|--------------------|--------|---------|
| Fidelia | | Spanish | Faithful one |
| Fiero | | Italian | Proud |
| Fifi | | French | Pet name for Josephine, God shall add |
| Filiberta | | Italian | Bright, shining |
| Filippa | | Italian | Lover of horses |
| Fiona | | Welsh | Fair |
| Fiore | | Italian | Flower |
| Fiorenze | | Italian | Flourishing |
| Fioretta | | Italian | Flourishing |
| Flamingo | | English | Beautiful pink bird |
| Flavia | | Italian | Golden |
| Fleur | | Latin | Flower |
| Fleurette | | French | Little flower |
| Flora | | Latin | Flower |
| Florence | | Place name | Italian city |
| Florence | | Latin | Blossoming |
| Florida | | Latin | Floral |
| Flower | | English | |
| Fortuna | | Latin | Fate |
| Fosca | | Italian | Dark |
| Fossetta | | French | Dimpled |
| Franca | | Italian | From France |
| Frances | | Latin | Free woman/from France |
| Francesca | | Italian | From France |
| Francine | | Italian | From France |
| Francisca | | Spanish | From France |
| Françoise | | French | From France |
| Frankie | | Latin | Free woman/from France |
| Frédérique | | French | Brave peacemaker |
| Freja | Freya, Freia | Scandinavian | Lady, goddess of love |

| Name | Alternate spellings | Origin | Meaning |
|------|---------------------|--------|---------|
| Frida | | Italian | She who has found peace |
| Frieda | Friede | German | Peace |
| Fuschia | | Latin | Flowering shrub |

| Name | Alternate spellings | Origin | Meaning |
|---|---|---|---|
| **G** | | | |
| Gabriel | | Hebrew | God is my strength, name of an archangel |
| Gabriella | | Italian | God is my strength |
| Gabrielle | | French | God is my strength |
| Gaea | | Greek | Earth goddess |
| Gaia | | Greek | Earth goddess |
| Gail | | Hebrew | Father's joy |
| Gala | | Russian | Calm |
| Galadriel | | Literary | *Lord of the Rings* by J. R. R. Tolkein |
| Galaxia | | Spanish | Galaxy |
| Galia | | Hebrew | God has redeemed |
| Galina | Galena | Russian | Calm |
| Galya | | Russian | Calm |
| Gardenia | | Latin | A flower |
| Garland | | French | Chain of blossoms |
| Gay | | French | Happy |
| Gayle | | Hebrew | Father's joy |
| Gazelle | | Latin | Antelope |
| Gedala | | Australian | The day |
| Geena | | American | From the farm |
| Gemella | | Italian | Twin sister |
| Gemini | | Latin | Twins, star sign and constellation |
| Gemma | | Latin | Precious stone |
| Geneva | | French | Junier tree |
| Geneviève | | French | Fair, blessed, soft |
| Georgia | | Greek | From the farm |
| Georgina | Georgia | Greek | Girl from the farm |

| Name | Alternate spellings | Origin | Meaning |
|---|---|---|---|
| Geraldina | | Italian | Precious stone |
| Gerd | Gerda | Scandinavian | Norse goddess of fertility |
| Germaine | | French | From Germany |
| Gertrude | Gertrud | German | Strong, spear |
| Ghada | | Arabic | Graceful |
| Ghalyela | | African | Precious |
| Ghera | | Australian | A gum leaf |
| Giada | | Italian | Jade |
| Gianna | | Italian | God is gracious |
| Gilda | | Italian | Sacrifice |
| Gilda | | German | Gilded |
| Gill | | Latin | Youthful |
| Gillian | | Latin | Youthful |
| Gimbya | | African | Princess |
| Gina | | Italian | God is gracious |
| Gina | | Greek | Girl from the farm |
| Ginevra | | Italian | Fair, blessed, smooth, soft |
| Ginny | | Latin | Short for Virginia or Ginevra |
| Giorgia | | Italian | From the farm |
| Giovanna | | Italian | God is gracious |
| Giselda | | Italian | Heroine |
| Giselle | Gisella | Italian | Heroine |
| Gita | | Sanskrit | A song |
| Gitana | | Spanish | Gypsy |
| Gladys | | Welsh | Country |
| Glen | | Scottish | Secluded valley |
| Glenda | | Welsh | Pure, holy |
| Glenys | | Welsh | Pure, holy |
| Gloria | | Latin | Glorious |
| Glynis | | Welsh | Pure, holy |
| Godiva | | Anglo-Saxon | Gift from God |
| Goldie | | Anglo-Saxon | From gold, precious metal |

| Name | Alternate spellings | Origin | Meaning |
|------|---------------------|--------|---------|
| Grace | | Latin | Graceful |
| Grainne | | Irish | From 'grain'. Daughter of an Irish king |
| Granya | | Irish | From 'grain'. Daughter of an Irish king |
| Grazia | | Italian | Grace |
| Graziella | | Italian | Grace |
| Greer | | Greek | Watchful mother |
| Greta | | Italian | Pearl |
| Gudrun | | Scandinavian | Divine, secret lore |
| Guendalina | | Italian | Blessed ring |
| Guinevere | | Welsh, Cornish | Fair, blessed, smooth, soft. Legendary wife of King Arthur |
| Gulara | | Australian | Moonlight |
| Gwaynten | | Cornish | Spring |
| Gwen | | Welsh | Fair, blessed |
| Gwendolin | | Welsh | Blessed ring |
| Gweneth | | Welsh | A region of Wales |
| Gweniver | | Welsh | Fair, blessed, smooth, soft. Legendary wife of King Arthur |
| Gwiryon | | Cornish | Sincere |
| Gwyn | | Welsh | Fair, blessed |
| Gwynder | | Cornish | Brightness |
| Gwynedd | | Welsh | A region of Wales |
| Gwyneth | | Welsh | A region of Wales |
| Gyneth | | Literary | *The Bridal of Triermain* by Sir Walter Scott |

| Name | Alternate spellings | Origin | Meaning |
|------|--------------------|---------|---------|
| | | | |

# H

| Name | Alternate spellings | Origin | Meaning |
|------|--------------------|---------|---------|
| Habiba | | Arabic | Beloved |
| Hadya | | Arabic | A leader or guide |
| Haiba | | African | Charm |
| Haifa | | Arabic | Slender |
| Hali | | | Happiness |
| Halla | | African | Unexpected gift |
| Halle | | Anglo-Saxon | Heroine |
| Hamida | | African | Gracious |
| Hana | | Arabic | Bliss, happiness |
| Hanna | | African | Happiness |
| Hannah | | Hebrew | Favoured by God, or graceful |
| Hanya | | Australian | A stork |
| Harmony | | Greek | In accord |
| Harper | | English | Harp player |
| Harriette | | French | Ruler of the home |
| Hasna | | Arabic | Beautiful |
| Hava | | Hebrew | Lovely |
| Havana | | Place name | Capital of Cuba |
| Hawlee | | American | From Hayley |
| Hayfa | | Arabic | Slender |
| Hayley | | Anglo-Saxon | From the hay meadow |
| Hazel | | Anglo-Saxon | Hazel tree |
| Heather | | Anglo-Saxon | Small heathland flower |
| Heaven | | English | |
| Hedia | | Hebrew | Voice of the Lord |
| Hedwig | Hedda | German | Contentious war |
| Heidi | | German | Noble |
| Helen | | Greek | Light/reed |
| Hélène | | French | Light of the sun |

| Name | Alternate spellings | Origin | Meaning |
|------|--------------------|--------|---------|
| Helga | | Anglo-Saxon | Blessed |
| Helga | | Scandinavian | Blessed, prosperous |
| Helima | | Arabic | Kind, gentle |
| Henriette | | French | Ruler of the home |
| Hermione | | Greek | Handsome one/earthy |
| Hermosa | | Spanish | Beautiful |
| Hertha | | Scandinavian | Norse goddess of fertility |
| Hester | | Greek | Star |
| Hika | | Pacific Islands | Daughter |
| Hilary | | Latin | Cheerful one |
| Hilda | Hilde | German | Battle |
| Hiriwa | | Pacific Islands | Silver |
| Hoku | | Pacific Islands | A star |
| Holly | | Anglo-Saxon | Holly tree |
| Honey | | English | Sweet food produced by bees |
| Honour | | Latin | Honourable one |
| Hope | | English | |
| Hortense | | French | Garden |
| Hulda | | Scandinavian | Sweet, lovable |
| Hyacinth | | Latin | A flower |
| Hypatia | | Greek | Intellectual |

| Name | Alternate spellings | Origin | Meaning |
|------|---------------------|--------|---------|
| **I** | | | |
| Ianthe | | Greek | Flower |
| Ida | | Italian | Island where Zeus was born |
| Idril | | Literary | *The Silmarillion* by J. R. R. Tolkein |
| Ikea | | Scandinavian | Smooth |
| Ileana | | Italian | Trojan |
| Ilse | | German | God is my vow |
| Imam | | Arabic | One who believes in God |
| Iman | | Arabic | Believer |
| Imelda | | Italian, Spanish | Light of the sun |
| Imena | | African | Dream |
| Imogen | | Latin | Like her mother |
| Ina | | Irish | Fire |
| Inas | | Pacific Islands | Wife of the moon |
| India | | Place name | Asian country |
| Indiana | | Place name | US state |
| Indigo | | | Deep blue |
| Indira | | Sanskrit | An alternative name for the wife of the god Vishnu |
| Ines | | Italian | Chaste |
| Inès | | French | Chaste |
| Infinity | | English | Eternity, endlessness |
| Ingrid | Inger | Scandinavian | From the norse fertility god, beautiful |
| Innocence | | English | Without crime or guile |
| Iola | | Greek | Dawn |
| Iolanthe | | Greek | Flower |

| Name | Alternate spellings | Origin | Meaning |
|------|---------------------|--------|---------|
| Ira | | Hebrew | Contented |
| Ireland | | Celebrity child | (Alec Baldwin and Kim Basinger) |
| Ireland | | Place name | Country |
| Irene | | Greek | Peace |
| Irina | | Russian | Peace |
| Iris | | Greek | Goddess of the rainbow |
| Irma | | Latin | Strong woman |
| Irmina | | Italian | Strong woman |
| Isa | | Scottish | Luminous |
| Isabel | | Spanish | Consecrated to God |
| Isabella | | Italian | Consecrated to God |
| Isabelle | | French | Consecrated to God |
| Isadora | | Greek | Gift of the Goddess Isis |
| Isidora | | Italian | Gift of the Goddess Isis |
| Isla | | Scottish | From the Hebridean Island, Islay |
| Isleta | | Spanish | Island |
| Isotta | | Italian | Protects with fire |
| Isra | | Arabic | Journeying by night |
| Israt | | Arabic | Affection |
| Iva | | Italian | God is gracious |
| Ivana | | Russian | God is gracious |
| Ivory | | English | Pale cream, material of elephant tusks |
| Ivy | | Anglo-Saxon | Plant name |
| Izzy | | American | Short for Isadora |

| Name | Alternate spellings | Origin | Meaning |
|------|---------------------|--------|---------|
| **J** | | | |
| Jacaranda | | Greek | A flower |
| Jacey | | American | Form of Jacinda (a flower) |
| Jacinda | | Greek | A flower |
| Jackie | | Hebrew | The one who replaces |
| Jacqueline | Jaqualine, Jackie | French | The supplanter |
| Jacquetta | Jacquette | French | The supplanter |
| Jada | | Anglo-Saxon | Semi-precious green gem |
| Jade | | Anglo-Saxon | Semi-precious green gem |
| Jadelyn | | American | Blend of Jade and Lynne |
| Jaela | Jael | Hebrew | Mountain goar |
| Jaime | Jamee | Hebrew | The one who replaces |
| Jaira | | Spanish | Jehova teaches |
| Jala | | Arabic | Clarity |
| Jalia | | African | Prominent |
| Jalila | Jalilah | Arabic | Great |
| Jalini | | Sanskrit | Lives next to the ocean |
| Jama | | Sanskrit | Daughter |
| Jamaica | | Place name | Caribbean island |
| Jamais | | French | Never |
| Jamal | | Arabic | Beautiful one |
| Jamee | Jaime | Hebrew | The one who replaces |
| Jamelia | | Arabic | Beautiful |
| Jamila | | Arabic | Beautiful |
| Jamilah | | Arabic | Beautiful |
| Jana | | Russian | God is gracious |
| Janan | | Arabic | Heart, soul |

| Name | Alternate spellings | Origin | Meaning |
|------|--------------------|--------|---------|
| Jane | | Hebrew | God is gracious |
| Janelle | | French | God is gracious |
| Janessa | | Literary | A mix of Jane and Vanessa, invented for *Guillver's Travels* by Jonathan Swift |
| Janet | | Scottish | God is gracious |
| Janice | | Hebrew | God is gracious |
| Janna | | Arabic | Fruit harvest |
| Jannali | | Australian | The moon |
| Jarita | | Sanskrit | A legendary bird |
| Jarnila | | Arabic | Beautiful |
| Jarrah | | Australian | A type of tree |
| Jasmine | | Arabic | A small fragrant white flower |
| Jaxine | | American | Form of Jacinda (a flower) |
| Jay | | American | Jaybird |
| Jaya | | Sanskrit | Victory |
| Jayden | Jaydon | Hebrew | Thankful |
| Jean | | French | God is gracious |
| Jeanne | | French | God is gracious |
| Jeannine | | French | God is gracious |
| Jehan | | Arabic | Beautiful flower |
| Jemima | | Hebrew | A dove |
| Jenna | | Cornish | God is Gracious |
| Jennifer | | Welsh | Fair, blessed, smooth, soft |
| Jenny | | Welsh | Fair, blessed, smooth, soft |
| Jensine | | Scandinavian | God is gracious |
| Jeri | | American | Appointed by God |
| Jessalyn | | American | Blend of Jessica and Lynn |
| Jesse | | Hebrew | God's gift |

| Name | Alternate spellings | Origin | Meaning |
|------|--------------------|--------|---------|
| Jessica | | Hebrew | Wealthy |
| Jewel | | English | Precious gem |
| Jezebel | | Hebrew | Impure |
| Jiba | | Australian | The moon |
| Jill | Gill | Latin | Youthful |
| Jillian | Jill | Latin | Youthful |
| Jira | | Arabic | Blood relative |
| Jirra | | Australian | A kangaroo |
| Joan | | Anglo-Saxon | God is gracious |
| Joanne | Jo, Joanna | Hebrew | God is gracious |
| Jocelyn | | American | Blend of Joyce and Lynn |
| Jodie | | Hebrew | Woman from Judea |
| Joelle | | Hebrew | The Lord is God |
| Jolan | | Hungarian | Violet |
| Jolene | | Hebrew | God will add |
| Jolie | | French | Happy |
| Joplin | | American | From surname of rock star, Janice Jopiln |
| Joquil | | Latin | A flower |
| Jora | | Hebrew | Autumn rain |
| Jordan | | Hebrew | Flowing down (as in the River Jordan) |
| Jordana | | Hebrew | Flowing down (as in the River Jordan) |
| Jordane | | Hebrew | Flowing down (as in the River Jordan) |
| Josephine | | Hebrew | God shall add |
| Josette | | French | God shall add |
| Josie | Jozie | Hebrew | From Josephine, God shall add |
| Joy | | Latin | Joyful |
| Joyce | | Latin | Joyful |

| Name | Alternate spellings | Origin | Meaning |
|------|---------------------|--------|---------|
| Juana | | Spanish | God is gracious |
| Juanita | | Spanish | God is gracious |
| Judith | | Hebrew | Woman from Judea |
| Judy | | Hebrew | Woman from Judea |
| Juillet | | French | July |
| Jules | | Latin | Youthful |
| Julia | | Latin | Youthful |
| Julie | | Latin | Youthful |
| Juliette | | French | Youthful |
| Jumelle | | French | Twin |
| Justine | | Latin | Fair, just |
| Jyoti | | Sanskrit | Light |

| Name | Alternate spellings | Origin | Meaning |
|------|---------------------|--------|---------|
| **K** | | | |
| Kacie | Kasey, Casey | Irish | Brave |
| Kadee | | Australian | Mother |
| Kadira | | Arabic | Powerful |
| Kadisha | | Hebrew | Holy |
| Kady | | American | Pure |
| Kaede | | Japanese | Maple leaf |
| Kaela | | Arabic | Beloved |
| Kai | | Pacific Islands | Sea |
| Kaimi | | Pacific Islands | The seeker |
| Kaimi | | Pacific Islands | Seeker |
| Kaisa | | Scandinavian | Pure |
| Kaitline | Caitlin | Irish | Pure |
| Kaiya | | Australian | A kind of spear |
| Kala | | Australian | Fire |
| Kalasia | | Pacific Islands | Graceful |
| Kalei | | Pacific Islands | Flower wreath |
| Kali | | Sanskrit | Black |
| Kalila | | Arabic | Beloved |
| Kalinda | | Sanskrit | The sea |
| Kalisa | Kalissa | American | Blend of Kate and Lisa |
| Kalpana | | Sanskrit | A fantasy |
| Kalyani | | Sanskrit | Lucky, beautiful |
| Kama | | Sanskrit | The golden one |
| Kamala | | Sanskrit | A loin |
| Kamaria | | African | Moonlight |
| Kameli | | Pacific Islands | Honey |
| Kamil | | Arabic | Perfect |
| Kamilah | | Arabic | The perfect one |
| Kamili | | African | Perfection |
| Kanani | | Pacific Islands | Beautiful |
| Kanti | | Sanskrit | Lovely |
| Kara | | Greek | Pure |
| Karen | Karin, Karon, Caron | Greek | Pure |

| Name | Alternate spellings | Origin | Meaning |
|------|---------------------|--------|---------|
| Karida | | Arabic | Virginal |
| Karima | | Arabic | Noble, generous |
| Karis | | Greek | Graceful |
| Karissa | | Greek | Grace |
| Karita | | Scandinavian | Charity |
| Karlotta | | Spanish | Little and strong |
| Katarina | | Scandinavian | Pure |
| Kate | Cate, Katie | Greek | Pure |
| Katharina | Katarina | German | Pure |
| Katharine | Kathy, Kate, Katie, Kath | Greek | Pure |
| Kathleen | Kathy, Kath | Scottish | Pure |
| Katinka | | Russian | Pure |
| Katya | | Russian | Pure |
| Kay | | Welsh | Joy |
| Kayla | | Hebrew | Like the Lord |
| Keana | | Irish | Beautiful |
| Kebira | | Arabic | Powerful |
| Keely | Keeley | Irish | Brave |
| Keisha | | African | Favourite |
| Kelly | | Irish | Intelligent |
| Kendra | | Anglo-Saxon | Knowing |
| Kenna | | American | Good looking |
| Kenya | | Russian | Innocent |
| Kerensa | | Cornish | Loving, affectionate |
| Kerra | | Cornish | Dearer |
| Kerry | Kerrie, Ceri | Irish | Dark haired, Irish county |
| Kesare | | Spanish | Hairy |
| Khalida | Khalidah | Arabic | Immortal |
| Kia | | African | Season's beginning |
| Kiah | | Australian | The beautiful place |
| Kiana | | American | Ancient |
| Kiera | Ciara | Irish, Welsh | Little dark one |
| Kim | | Anglo-Saxon | Chief, ruler |

| Name | Alternate spellings | Origin | Meaning |
|---|---|---|---|
| Kimberley | Kim | Anglo-Saxon | Chief, ruler |
| Kiri | | Pacific Islands | Tree bark |
| Kirsten | | Scandinavian | Follower of Christ |
| Kirstin | | Scottish | Christian |
| Kirsty | Kirstie | Scottish | Christian |
| Kit | | Greek | Bearer of Christ |
| Kitten | | English | Baby cat |
| Kodi | | American | Helpful |
| Kohia | | Pacific Islands | An exotic flower |
| Kristen | | Scandinavian | Follower of Christ |
| Krysanthe | | Greek | From the flower, Chrysanthenum |
| Krystal | | American | Clear, brilliant glass |
| Kumari | | Sanskrit | A girl |
| Kura | | Pacific Islands | Red |
| Kyle | | Irish | Attractive |
| Kylie | | Australian | Boomerang |
| Kyra | Kyri, Kyrie | Greek | Noble |

| Name | Alternate spellings | Origin | Meaning |
|------|---------------------|--------|---------|

## L

| Name | Alternate spellings | Origin | Meaning |
|------|---------------------|--------|---------|
| Lakshmi | | Sanskrit | The Hindu goddess of beauty and wealth |
| Lalita | | Sanskrit | Playful, charming |
| Lamorna | | Place name | Cornish fishing village |
| Lana | | Russian | Little rock or handsome |
| Lani | | Pacific Islands | The sky |
| Lara | | Latin | Shining |
| Larisa | | Russian | Citadel |
| Larissa | | Russian | Citadel |
| Latifa | | Arabic | Kind and gentle |
| Latisha | | Latin | Joy |
| Latoya | | Spanish | Victory |
| Laura | | Latin | Crowned with laurels |
| Laure | | French | Crowned with laurels |
| Laurel | | Latin | Crowned with laurels |
| Lauren | | Latin | Crowned with laurels |
| Lavender | | Hebrew | Blue, purple, fragrant flower |
| Lavinia | | Latin | Famous Roman Princess |
| Layla | | African | Born at night |
| Lea | | Italian | Weary or ruler |
| Leaf | | Anglo-Saxon | Foliage |
| Leah | | Hebrew | Weary or ruler |
| Leala | | French | Loyal one |
| Leandra | | Latin | Like a lioness |
| Leda | | Greek | A queen, mother of Helen of Troy |

| Name | Alternate spellings | Origin | Meaning |
|------|---------------------|--------|---------|
| Lee | Leigh | Anglo-Saxon | From the meadow |
| Leela | | Sanskrit | Playful |
| Leigh | Lee | Anglo-Saxon | Meadow |
| Leila | | Arabic | Dark as the night |
| Lelia | | Italian | Playful |
| Lenita | | Latin | Gentle |
| Leona | | American | Like a lion |
| Leonida | | Italian | Like a lion |
| Leonie | | Latin | Lioness |
| Leonoro | | Italian | Leader |
| Leora | | Greek | Light |
| Lesbia | | Greek | From the island of Lesbos |
| Lesley | Leslie | Scottish | From the grey fortress |
| Letitia | | Latin | Happiness |
| Letizia | | Italian | Happy |
| Lewanna | Lewana | Hebrew | The moon |
| Lexie | | Greek | Short for Alexis |
| Lia | | Italian | Hard worker |
| Liani | | Spanish | Youthful |
| Libby | Libbie | Italian | God is my vow |
| Libera | | Italian | Free |
| Liberty | Libby | Latin | Free |
| Libra | | Latin | Scales, star sign and constellation |
| Licia | | Italian | From Lisia (in Asia Minor) |
| Lidia | Lydia | Italian | From Lidia (region) |
| Liese | | German | God is my vow |
| Lila | Lyla | Arabic | Night |
| Lilac | | Anglo-Saxon | A flower |
| Lilah | | Hebrew | The beautiful temptress |

| Name | Alternate spellings | Origin | Meaning |
| --- | --- | --- | --- |
| Liliana | | Italian | From Lily, the flower, symbol of purity and peace |
| Lilith | | Arabic | Dark as night |
| Lillian | | Anglo-Saxon | From the lilac flower |
| Lilliom | | Literary | *Lilliom* by Ferenc Molnar |
| Lily | Lilly | Anglo-Saxon | The flower, symbolic of purity and peace |
| Lina | | Arabic | Tender |
| Linda | | Italian | Pretty girl |
| Linette | | French | A bird |
| Linn | | Anglo-Saxon | Waterfall |
| Lisa | | Hebrew | Consecrated to God |
| Lisbet | Lisbeth, Lisabetta | Hebrew | Consecrated to God |
| Lisha | | African | Mysterious |
| Lissa | | Greek | Honey bee |
| Liv | | Scandinavian | Life |
| Livia | | Italian | Crown |
| Liz | Lizzy, Lizzie | Hebrew | Consecrated to God |
| Liza | | Hebrew | Consecrated to God |
| Lizaveta | | Russian | Consecrated to God |
| Llewella | | Welsh | Like a lion |
| Lois | | Anglo-Saxon | Famous warrior |
| Lona | | Spanish | Like a lion |
| Lorelei | | German | Mythical siren of the River Rhine |
| Lorena | | Italian | Laurel |
| Lorenza | | Italian | Crowned with laurels |

| Name | Alternate spellings | Origin | Meaning |
|------|---------------------|--------|---------|
| Lori | | Latin | Crowned with laurels |
| Lorna | | Literary | From the novel *Lorna Doone* by R. D. Blackmore |
| Lorraine | | French | Region of France |
| Lotte | | German | Strong, free |
| Lotus | | Latin | A flower |
| Louise | Louisa | French | Famous warrior |
| Lourdes | | Spanish | After Lourdes, the famous site of pilgrimage |
| Love | | English | |
| Loveday | | Anglo-Saxon | |
| Lovelace | | English | Surname used as a first name |
| Lovisa | | Scandinavian | Famous warrior |
| Lowenna | | Cornish | Joy |
| Lowri | | Welsh | From the laurel tree |
| Luana | | Pacific Islands | Enjoyment |
| Lucetta | | Spanish | Light |
| Lucia | | Italian, Spanish | Light |
| Luciana | Lucy | Italian | Light |
| Lucilla | Lucille | Latin | Light |
| Lucinda | Lucy | Latin | Light |
| Lucky | | American | Fortunate |
| Lucrezia | | Italian | Wealthy |
| Lucy | | Latin | Pet form of Lucinda or Lucille, light |
| Ludmila | | Russian | Favour of the people |
| Luigia | | Italian, Spanish | Famous warrior |
| Luise | | German | Famous warrior |
| Luisella | | Italian | Famous warrior |

| Name | Alternate spellings | Origin | Meaning |
|------|---------------------|--------|---------|
| Lujuana | | Spanish | Famous warrior |
| Lulu | | German | Famous warrior |
| Luna | | Latin | The moon |
| Lunar | | Anglo-Saxon | Of the moon |
| Lydia | Lidia | Greek | Woman from Lydia, cultured |
| Lyla | | Arabic | Night |
| Lyn | | Anglo-Saxon | Waterfall |
| Lynda | | Spanish | Pretty |
| Lyndsey | Lyndsay | Anglo-Saxon | Lincoln's marsh |
| Lynette | | Welsh | Idol |
| Lynn | Lynne, Lynna | Anglo-Saxon | Waterfall |
| Lynx | | English | Large, wild cat |
| Lyra | | Greek | Lyre player. Star sign and constellation |
| Lysander | | Greek | Liberator |
| Lysandra | | Greek | Liberator |
| Lyuba | | Russian | Love |

| Name | Alternate spellings | Origin | Meaning |
|------|---------------------|--------|---------|
| **M** | | | |
| Mabel | | French | Pretty girl |
| Macey | Macee, Masey | American | Bitter |
| Maddalena | | Italian | From the village of Magdala |
| Madelaine | | Hebrew | From the village of Magdala |
| Madhuri | | Sanskrit | Sweet |
| Madison | | Anglo-Saxon | Son of Matthew |
| Madonna | | Anglo-Saxon | From 'My lady' the Virgin Mary |
| Madra | | Spanish | Mother |
| Maeve | | Irish | Intoxicating. Famous Irish queen |
| Magda | | German | From Mary Magdalene |
| Magdalene | | German | From Mary Magdalene |
| Magenta | | Anglo-Saxon | Deep, bright pink, purple |
| Maggie | Mags | Greek | Pearl |
| Mahala | | Arabic | Tender |
| Mahina | | Pacific Islands | The moon |
| Mai | | French | May |
| Maia | | Latin | Bitter |
| Maire | | Irish | Bitter |
| Maisha | | African | Life |
| Maisie | | Anglo-Saxon | Short for Margaret, pearl |
| Malak | | Arabic | An angel. |
| Malati | | Sanskrit | A jasmine flower. |
| Malaya | | Place name | Stems from the Tamil word meaning hill town |

| Name | Alternate spellings | Origin | Meaning |
|------|---------------------|--------|---------|
| Malika | | Arabic | Lady, Mistress |
| Malika | | African | Queen |
| Malory | Mallory | French | Luckless |
| Mani | | Sanskrit | A gem |
| Manjusha | | Sanskrit | A box of jewels |
| Manon | | French | Bitter |
| Manuela | | Italian, Spanish | God is with us |
| Mara | | Latin | Bitter |
| Marcella | | Latin | Of Mars, God of war, warrior |
| Marcelle | | French | Warrior |
| Marcia | | Latin | Of Mars, God of war, warrior |
| Mardi | | French | Tuesday |
| Mareta | Marita | Italian | Bitter |
| Margaret | Maggie | Greek | Pearl |
| Margaux | | French | Pearl |
| Margeurite | | Latin | Pearl, also a flower |
| Margot | | French | Pearl |
| Maria | Marie, Mariah | Latin | Bitter |
| Marian | | Anglo-Saxon | Sea of bitterness |
| Marianna | | Italian | Sea of bitterness |
| Marianne | | French | Bitter |
| Maribel | | Spanish | Blend of Mary, bitter and Belle, beautiful |
| Marie | | French | Bitter |
| Marigold | | Latin | A flower |
| Marina | | Latin | Of the sea |
| Marine | | French | Of the sea |
| Mariposa | | Spanish | Butterfly |
| Mariquita | | Spanish | Bitter |
| Marisa | Marissa | Italian | Bitter |
| Marita | Mareta | Spanish | Bitter |
| Mariya | Mariah | Russian | Bitter |
| Marjorie | Madge, Marj | French | Pearl |

| Name | Alternate spellings | Origin | Meaning |
|------|---------------------|--------|---------|
| Marlene | | German | From Mary, bitter and Magdalene |
| Marlon | | Anglo-Saxon | Little hawk |
| Marna | Marnie | Scandinavian | Of the sea |
| Marsha | | Latin | Of Mars, God of war, warrior |
| Marta | | Italian, Spanish | Mistress of the house |
| Martha | | Anglo-Saxon | Mistress of the house |
| Martina | | Italian | Warrior |
| Martine | | Latin | Of Mars, God of war, warrior |
| Maru | | Pacific Islands | Gentle |
| Marvelle | | French | Miracle |
| Mary | | Latin | Bitter |
| Maryse | | French | Bitter |
| Marzia | | Italian | Bitter |
| Matana | | Arabic | Gift |
| Mathilde | Mathilda, Tilly | French | Strong in battle |
| Matilda | Tilly | Anglo-Saxon | Strong in battle |
| Matilde | | Italian | Strong in battle |
| Maud | | Anglo-Saxon | Mightly maiden of battle |
| Maureen | Mo | Irish | Bitter |
| Mauve | | English | Pale purple |
| Maxine | | Latin | The greatest |
| Maya | | Latin | The great one |
| Maysa | | Arabic | Graceful |
| McKayla | | American | Fiery |
| Medina | | Arabic | A city in Saudi Arabia |
| Medora | | Place name | US town |
| Meena | | Sanskrit | Fish |
| Megan | | Irish | Pearl |
| Mel | | Greek | Dark one |
| Melanie | | Greek | Dark one |

| Name | Alternate spellings | Origin | Meaning |
|------|---------------------|--------|---------|
| Melek | | Arabic | An angel |
| Melina | | Greek | Gentle |
| Melinda | Mel | Greek | Honey |
| Melisenda | | Spanish | Honey bee |
| Melissa | | Greek | Honey bee |
| Melody | | Greek | Tune, song |
| Melosa | | Spanish | Honey bee |
| Mercedes | | Spanish | Wages, reward |
| Meredith | | Welsh | Great ruler |
| Merete | | Scandinavian | Pearl |
| Merise | | French | Wild cherry |
| Meryl | | Latin | Blackbird |
| Mia | | Scandinavian | Bitterly-wanted child |
| Michaela | | Hebrew | Like the Lord |
| Michela | | Italian | Like God |
| Michèle | | French | Like God |
| Michelina | | Italian | Like God |
| Michelle | | Hebrew | Like the Lord |
| Micky | | Hebrew | Like the Lord |
| Mignon | | French | Petite |
| Mikhaila | | Russian | Like God |
| Mildred | | Anglo-Saxon | Gentle advisor |
| Milena | | Russian | Gracious |
| Milly | Millie | Anglo-Saxon | Short for Mildred, gentle advisor |
| Mina | | German | Love |
| Minerva | | Latin | Goddess of wisdom |
| Mira | | Italian | Aim |
| Mirabelle | | Latin | Lovely |
| Miranda | | Latin | Admired one |
| Mirella | Mirelle | Italian | Admired one |
| Mireya | | Spanish | Admired one |
| Miriam | | Latin | Bitter |
| Misha | | Russian | Like God |

| Name | Alternate spellings | Origin | Meaning |
|------|---------------------|--------|---------|
| Mitzi | | German | Bitterly-wanted child |
| Mohana | | Sanskrit | The enchantress |
| Moira | | Irish | Bitter |
| Molly | | Irish | Short for Moira, bitter |
| Mona | | Irish | Noble |
| Money | | English | Cash |
| Monica | | Latin | Advisor |
| Monique | | French | Advisor |
| Montana | | Place name | US state |
| Moon | | Anglo-Saxon | Sphere that orbits Earth |
| Mora | Maura | Spanish | Bitter |
| Morenwyn | | Cornish | Fair maiden |
| Morgana | | Welsh | Bright sea dweller |
| Morna | | Irish | Loved |
| Morwenna | | Cornish | Maiden |
| Moyna | | Irish | Noble |
| Muna | | Arabic | A wish |
| Munira | | Arabic | The luminous one |
| Muriel | | Arabic | Myrhh |
| Musique | | French | Music |
| Myiesha | | Arabic | Life's blessing |
| Myra | | Latin | Fragrant ointment |
| Myrtle | | Greek | Plant name |

| Name | Alternate spellings | Origin | Meaning |
|------|---------------------|--------|---------|

## N

| Name | Alternate spellings | Origin | Meaning |
|------|---------------------|--------|---------|
| Naava | | Hebrew | Delightful girl |
| Nabila | | Arabic | Noble |
| Nada | Nadya, Naadia | Arabic | Generous |
| Nadia | Naadia, Nadya | Italian | Hope |
| Nadine | Nadeen | Russian | Dancer |
| Nadira | | Arabic | Precious |
| Nadya | Nadia, Naadia | Russian | Hope |
| Nafeeza | | Arabic | Precious |
| Nagini | | Sanskrit | Mythical snake-like beauties |
| Nalini | | Sanskrit | Lovely |
| Nancy | | Irish | Generous woman |
| Nanette | | French | Giving |
| Nani | | Pacific Islands | Beautiful |
| Nanna | | Scandinavian | Daring |
| Naomi | | Hebrew | Pleasant |
| Narcissa | | Greek | Self-love |
| Nastasia | | Russian | Resurrection |
| Nat | | Latin | God's gift |
| Natalia | | Italian | Born at Christmas |
| Natalie | | Latin | God's gift |
| Natascia | | Italian | Born at Christmas |
| Natasha | | Russian | Born at Christmas |
| Nathalie | | French | God's gift |
| Nawal | | Arabic | A gift |
| Nazirah | | Arabic | Equal |
| Nebraska | | American | American state |

| Name | Alternate spellings | Origin | Meaning |
|------|---------------------|--------|---------|
| Neera | | Italian | Pet name for Deyanira, devastating |
| Nella | | Italian | Light of the sun |
| Nelly | | Anglo-Saxon | Pet name for Helen, light of the sun |
| Nereida | | Greek | Sea nymph |
| Nerissa | | Greek | Sea nymph |
| Neroli | | Greek | Orangle blossom flower |
| Nerys | | Welsh | Noble |
| Netta | | Scottish | Champion |
| Nettie | | French | Gentle |
| Neva | | Spanish | Snow |
| Nevada | | Spanish | Snow-capped |
| Neve | | Italian | Snow |
| Nia | Nyah | Irish | Beauty, brightness, daughter of Celtic sea god |
| Niamh | | Irish | Beauty, brightness, daughter of Celtic sea god |
| Nicky | Niki, Nikki | Greek | Victory of the people |
| Nicola | Nichola | Greek | Victory of the people |
| Nicole | | French | Victory of the people |
| Nicoletta | | Italian | Victory of the people |
| Nike | | Greek | Goddess of victory |
| Nikita | | Greek | Unconquered people |
| Nimah | | Arabic | Blessing |
| Nina | | Hebrew | Beautiful |

| Name | Alternate spellings | Origin | Meaning |
|------|---------------------|--------|---------|
| Nissa | | Hebrew | Symbolic |
| Noelle | | French | Christmas |
| Nola | | Latin | Sensual |
| Noor | | Arabic | Light |
| Nora | | Italian | From the north |
| Noreen | | Latin | Acknowledges others |
| Norma | | Anglo-Saxon | From the north |
| Novella | | Italian | Daughter of the clouds |
| Noya | | Arabic | Beautiful |
| Numa | | Spanish | Delightful |
| Nydia | | Latin | Home-maker |
| Nymphadora | | Greek | Gift of the nymphs |
| Nyx | | Greek | Lively |

| Name | Alternate spellings | Origin | Meaning |
|------|---------------------|--------|---------|
| **O** | | | |
| Ocean | | Anglo-Saxon | Vast body of water |
| Océane | | French | The ocean |
| Octavia | | Latin | Eighth child |
| Odessa | | Greek | Journey |
| Odetta | | Italian | Wealthy |
| Odette | | French | Wealthy |
| Ofra | Ofrah | Hebrew | Fawn or lively girl |
| Ola | | Scandinavian | Gold |
| Olaide | | American | Lovely |
| Olalla | | Spanish | Well-spoken |
| Oleander | | Greek | A flower |
| Olga | | Italian | Blessed |
| Olino | | Spanish | Scented |
| Olive | | Anglo-Saxon | A tree, colour and food |
| Olivia | | Latin | From the olive tree |
| Olivie | | French | From the olive tree |
| Olwen | | Welsh | Magical |
| Oma | | Arabic | Long-lived |
| Omesha | | African | Splendid |
| Onda | | Italian | Wave |
| Oni | | African | Desired child |
| Opal | | Sanskrit | Precious |
| Ophelia | | Greek | A helper |
| Ophrah | | Hebrew | Fawn or lively girl |
| Oprah | | Greek | Fawn. Name of celebrity chat-show host, Oprah Winfrey |
| Ora | | Pacific Islands | Life |
| Ora | | Anglo-Saxon | Sea coast |

| Name | Alternate spellings | Origin | Meaning |
|------|---------------------|--------|---------|
| Orana | | Australian | The moon |
| Orene | | French | Nurturing |
| Orin | | Welsh | Feisty |
| Orinthia | | Literary | *The Apple Cart* by George Bernard Shaw |
| Orissa | | Place name | A region in India |
| Orla | | Irish | Golden princess |
| Ortensia | | Italian | She who is in the garden |
| Ozara | | Hebrew | Treasured |

| Name | Alternate spellings | Origin | Meaning |
|------|---------------------|--------|---------|
| **P** | | | |
| Pacifica | | Spanish | Peaceful |
| Padma | | Sanskrit | A lotus |
| Page | | French | Sharp |
| Paisley | | Scottish | Patterned |
| Paka | | African | Cat |
| Palmira | | Italian | Palm tree |
| Paloma | | Spanish | Dove |
| Pamela | | Greek | Sweet as honey |
| Pandora | | Greek | Gifted girl |
| Pangari | | Australian | Soulful |
| Pansy | | Latin | A flower |
| Paola | | Italian | Small |
| Paradise | | English | Perfect place |
| Paris | | Greek | French city |
| Parminder | | Sanskrit | Attractive |
| Parvati | | Sanskrit | The daughter of the mountain |
| Pascale | | French | Born at Easter |
| Pat | | Latin | Noble |
| Patia | | Spanish | Most high |
| Patience | | English | |
| Patricia | Pat, Trish, Trisha | Latin | Noble |
| Patsy | Pat | Latin | Noble |
| Paula | | Latin | Small |
| Paulette | | French | Small |
| Pauline | | French | Small |
| Pax | | Latin | Goddess of peace |
| Peace | | Anglo-Saxon | Calm or tranquil |
| Peach | | Anglo-Saxon | A fruit |
| Peaches | | Celebrity child | (Paula Yates and Bob Geldof) |
| Pearl | | Anglo-Saxon | Luminous jewel found in oysters shells |

| Name | Alternate spellings | Origin | Meaning |
|------|---------------------|--------|---------|
| Pebbles | | Anglo-Saxon | Small rounded stones |
| Peggy | | Anglo-Saxon | Pearl |
| Pelagia | | Greek | From the sea |
| Penelope | | Greek | The weaver |
| Penny | | Greek | Short for Penelope, the weaver |
| Pepa | | Spanish | God shall add |
| Pepita | | Spanish | God shall add |
| Peppy | | American | From Pepa, God shall add |
| Perla | | Spanish, Italian | Pearl |
| Persia | | Place name | Ancient region of the Middle East |
| Peta | | Greek | From Pepita, God shall add |
| Petal | | Anglo-Saxon | Part of a flower |
| Petra | | Place name | Ancient city in Jordan |
| Petronilla | | Italian | Yokel |
| Petula | | Anglo-Saxon | Rock |
| Petunia | | Anglo-Saxon | A flower |
| Philippa | | Greek | Lover of horses |
| Philippine | | French | Lover of horses |
| Philly | | Greek | From Philippa, lover of horses |
| Philomena | | Greek | Lover of the moon |
| Phoebe | | Greek | Light |
| Phoenix | | Greek | Rebirth. Mythical bird who was reborn in fire |
| Phyliss | | Greek | A branch |
| Phyllida | | Greek | Lovely |
| Pia | | Italian | Pious, dutiful |

| Name | Alternate spellings | Origin | Meaning |
|------|--------------------|--------|---------|
| Pierah | | Australian | The moon |
| Pilar | | Spanish | Strength |
| Pink | | Anglo-Saxon | A colour |
| Piper | | Anglo-Saxon | Pipe player |
| Pippa | Pip, Pippy | Greek | From Philippa, lover of horses |
| Pisces | | Greek | Fishes. Star sign and constellation |
| Pixie | | Anglo-Saxon | A mythical, mischievous fairylike creature |
| Plum | | Anglo-Saxon | A fruit |
| Polina | | Russian | From the Greek God Apollo |
| Polly | | Anglo-Saxon | From Molly |
| Pomona | | Latin | Roman goddess of fruit trees |
| Poppy | | Anglo-Saxon | A red flower |
| Porsche | | Latin | Giving, high-minded |
| Portia | Porscha | Latin | From a Roman tribe |
| Precious | | English | Valuable, beloved |
| Prema | | Sanskrit | Love, affection |
| Presley | | Anglo-Saxon | Priests meadow |
| Primrose | | Latin | First rose |
| Princess Tiaamii | | Celebrity child | (Katie Price and Peter Andre) |
| Priscilla | | Italian | Ancient |
| Priya | | Sanskrit | Beloved |
| Providence | | Anglo-Saxon | God will provide |
| Prudence | | Latin | Careful |
| Prunella | | Latin | Little plum |
| Psyche | | Greek | Of the soul |
| Pulika | | African | Obedient |
| Purnima | | Sanskrit | The night of the full moon |

| Name | Alternate spellings | Origin | Meaning |
|------|---------------------|--------|---------|

## Q

| Name | Alternate spellings | Origin | Meaning |
|------|---------------------|--------|---------|
| Qadira | | Arabic | Powerful |
| Qamra | | Arabic | Moon |
| Qing | | Chinese | Blue |
| Queenie | | Anglo-Saxon | Queen |
| Quenna | | Anglo-Saxon | Queen |
| Questa | | Latin | Seeker |
| Quinby | | Scandinavian | Living like royalty |
| Quinella | | Latin | Twice as pretty |
| Quisha | | African | Spiritual and physical beauty |
| Quita | | Latin | Peaceful |

| Name | Alternate spellings | Origin | Meaning |
|------|---------------------|--------|---------|
| **R** | | | |
| Rabbit | | American | The animal! |
| Rabi | | Arabic | Harvest |
| Rachael | Rachel | Hebrew | Ewe. Biblical wife of Jacob and mother of Joseph |
| Radella | | Anglo-Saxon | Elfin advisor |
| Radha | | Sanskrit | The name of a Hindu goddess |
| Rae | | Anglo-Saxon | Deer |
| Rafaella | | Hebrew | God has healed |
| Rafiya | | African | Dignified |
| Rain | | Latin | Ruler |
| Raina | | Russian | Queen |
| Rainbow | | English | Arch of colours |
| Raindrop | | Anglo-Saxon | Drop of water that falls from the sky |
| Raisa | | African | Exalted |
| Raissa | | French | Believer |
| Raja | | Arabic | Hope |
| Rajani | | Sanskrit | Dark, of the night |
| Rakel | | Scandinavian | Ewe |
| Ramona | | Anglo-Saxon | Beautiful |
| Rana | | Arabic | Beautiful |
| Randi | Randy | Anglo-Saxon | Wolf shield |
| Rangi | | Pacific Islands | Heaven |
| Rani | | Sanskrit | A queen |
| Raphaella | | Hebrew | Divine healer |
| Rashida | | Arabic | Righteous |
| Rati | | Sanskrit | Love |
| Raven | | English | Large, black bird |
| Raya | | Russian | Relaxed |

| Name | Alternate spellings | Origin | Meaning |
|------|---------------------|--------|---------|
| Razia | | Hebrew | Secretive |
| Rebecca | Rebekah, Becca, Becky | Hebrew | Heifer or knotted chord. Biblical wife of Isaac |
| Reenie | | Greek | Peace-loving |
| Regina | | Latin | Queen, offical name of Queen Elizabeth II |
| Reiko | | Japanese | Gratitude |
| Rena | | Hebrew | Song |
| Renata | | Italian | Reborn |
| Rene | | Latin | Reborn |
| Renée | | French | Born again |
| Renite | | Latin | Stubborn |
| Rewa | | Pacific Islands | Slender |
| Rexanne | | Anglo-Saxon | Gracious king |
| Rhea | | Greek | Stream or mother |
| Rhianna | | Welsh | Pure |
| Rhiannon | | Welsh | Nymph, goddess |
| Rhoda | | Greek | Rose |
| Rhonda | | Place name | Rhonda valley in Wales |
| Rhonwen | | Welsh | Fair haired |
| Ria | | Spanish | River |
| Rica | | Spanish | Celestial |
| Richelle | | American | From the word rich |
| Ricky | | American | Pet name for Erica or Frederica |
| Ridhaa | | African | Goodwill |
| Rina | Rinah | Hebrew | Complete joy |
| Ripple | | Anglo-Saxon | Distrubance in smooth water |
| Rita | | Italian | Short form of Margarita, pearl |
| Riva | | Italian | Shore |

| Name | Alternate spellings | Origin | Meaning |
|------|---------------------|--------|---------|
| Roberta | | Italian | Bright fame |
| Robin | | Anglo-Saxon | Bright fame |
| Robina | | Italian | Bright fame |
| Roche | | French | Rock |
| Rochelle | | French | Little rock |
| Rohana | | Sanskrit | Sandalwood |
| Roisin | | Irish | Rose |
| Roksana | | Russian | Dawn |
| Romilda | | Italian | Heroine |
| Romilly | | Latin | Wanderer |
| Romola | | Italian | From Romilia |
| Romy | | German | Short form of Rosemary |
| Rona | | Scandinavian | Mighty power |
| Ros | | Irish | Rose |
| Rosa | | Latin | Rose |
| Rosalia | Rosa, Roz | Latin | Beautiful rose |
| Rosalie | Rosa, Roz | Latin | Beautiful rose |
| Rosalind | Rosa, Roz | Latin | Beautiful rose |
| Rosalyn | Roz | Latin | Beautiful rose |
| Rosamond | Rosamund | Latin | Pure rose |
| Rosanna | | Italian | Rose, grace |
| Rosaria | | Italian | Rosary |
| Rosario | | Spanish | Rosary |
| Rose | | Latin | The flower |
| Rosemary | | Latin | from the herb |
| Rosenwyn | | Cornish | Fair rose |
| Rosetta | | Italian | Rose |
| Rosie | | Latin | The flower |
| Rosina | | Italian | Rose |
| Rosita | | Italian, Spanish | Rose |
| Rossana | | Italian | Rose, grace |
| Rosslyn | | Welsh | Moorland lake |
| Rowena | | Latin | From the Rowan tree |
| Roxanna | Roxana, Roxy | Arabic | Beautiful dawn |

| Name | Alternate spellings | Origin | Meaning |
|------|---------------------|--------|---------|
| Roxanne | Roxy | Arabic | Beautiful dawn |
| Roxy | | Arabic | Beautiful dawn |
| Royale | | French | Regal |
| Rubena | | Hebrew | See, a son |
| Ruby | | Latin | Red, precious stone |
| Rudy | | German | Sly |
| Rue | | English | Regret |
| Rufina | | Italian | Red haired |
| Rukmini | | Sanskrit | The wife of Lord Krishna |
| Rula | | Russian | Sovereign |
| Runa | | Scandinavian | Secret lore |
| Ruth | | Hebrew | Beautiful and compassionate |

| Name | Alternate spellings | Origin | Meaning |
|------|---------------------|--------|---------|
| **S** | | | |
| Saada | | African | Helper |
| Sabah | | Arabic | Morning |
| Sabbia | | Italian | Sand |
| Sabina | | Latin | From the Sabine tribe from Roman Italy |
| Sabine | | Latin | From the Sabine tribe from Roman Italy |
| Sabira | Sabirah | Arabic | Patience |
| Sabra | | African | Patience |
| Sabrina | | Welsh | In Celtic legend the girl who gave her name to the River Severn |
| Sacha | Sasha | Russian | Defender of mankind |
| Sadhbh | | Irish | Sweet |
| Sadie | | Hebrew | Princess |
| Safari | | African | Long journey |
| Saffron | | Arabic | A spice |
| Safia | | Arabic | Pure one |
| Safran | | French | Saffron |
| Saga | | Scandinavian | Sensual |
| Sahar | | Arabic | Dawn |
| Sahara | | Arabic | Desert |
| Saida | | Arabic | Lucky |
| Saison | | French | Season |
| Sakinah | | Arabic | Divine tranquillity |
| Salima | | Arabic | Safe |
| Salimah | | Arabic | Safe |
| Sally | | Hebrew | Princess |
| Salma | | Literary | Beautiful appearance |

| Name | Alternate spellings | Origin | Meaning |
|------|---------------------|--------|---------|
| Salome | | Hebrew | Peace |
| Salome | | Hebrew | Peace |
| Salvadora | | Spanish | Saved |
| Salwa | | Arabic | Comfort |
| Samantha | Sam, Sammy | Greek | Listener of God |
| Samara | | Hebrew | Guarded by God |
| Samirah | | Arabic | Lively companion |
| Samma | | Arabic | Sky |
| Samuela | | Hebrew | God has heard |
| Sana | | Arabic | Radiant |
| Sandia | | Spanish | Defender of mankind |
| Sandra | | Italian | Defender of mankind |
| Sandrea | | Greek | Defender of mankind |
| Sandy | Sandie | Greek | Defender of mankind |
| Sanila | | Sanskrit | Full of praise |
| Santa | | Italian | Saintly |
| Santina | | Italian | Saintly |
| Sapphire | | Greek | A precious deep blue gem |
| Sara | | Italian | Princess |
| Sarah | | Hebrew | A princess. Abraham's wife in the Bible |
| Saree | | Arabic | Noble |
| Sarisha | | Sanskrit | Charming |
| Saroja | | Sanskrit | Born in a lake |
| Sasha | | Russian | Defender of mankind |
| Saskia | | Scandinavian | Defender of mankind |
| Sassa | | Scandinavian | Divine beauty |
| Satine | Satin | French | Shining |
| Savanna | | Spanish | Grassy plain |

| Name | Alternate spellings | Origin | Meaning |
|------|---------------------|--------|---------|
| Savannah | | Place name | US city |
| Sawsan | | Arabic | Lily of the valley |
| Scarlet | | Anglo-Saxon | Deep, dark red |
| Scout | | Celebrity child | (Demi Moore and Bruce Willis) |
| Sea | | American | |
| Sean | | Irish | God is gracious |
| Seema | | Hebrew | Treasured |
| Selena | Selina | Greek | Goddess of the moon |
| Selene | | Greek | Goddess of the moon |
| Selma | | Literary | Beautiful appearance |
| Senara | | Cornish | From St Zennor |
| Serena | | Latin | Calm, serene |
| Serendipity | | English | Making lucky discoveries by accident |
| Serenity | | Latin | Calm, peaceful |
| Sevilla | | Spanish | From Seville |
| Shadow | | English | |
| Shae | | Hebrew | Sky |
| Shahira | | Arabic | Famous |
| Shakira | | Arabic | Thankful |
| Shakti | | Sanskrit | The powerful one |
| Shakuntala | | Sanskrit | A bird |
| Shamra | | Sanskrit | Adorable |
| Shance | | French | Grateful |
| Shane | | Irish | God is gracious |
| Shania | | American | Native American for 'on my way' |
| Shannon | | Irish | God is gracious |
| Shanti | | Sanskrit | The tranquil one |
| Sharmila | | Sanskrit | The protected one |

| Name | Alternate spellings | Origin | Meaning |
|---|---|---|---|
| Sharon | | Hebrew | A flat plain |
| Shauny | | Irish | God is gracious |
| Shavon | | Irish | Devout |
| Shawnee | | American | Native American Indian tribe |
| Shea | | Irish | Soft beauty |
| Sheela | | Sanskrit | Of good character |
| Sheena | | Hebrew | God is gracious |
| Sheila | | Latin | Blind |
| Shelah | | Hebrew | Request |
| Shelby | | Anglo-Saxon | Sheltered town |
| Shelley | | Anglo-Saxon | From the ledge meadow |
| Sher | | Sanskrit | The beloved one |
| Sherilyn | | American | Blend of Cheryl (petite and free) and Marilyn (bitter, pretty) |
| Sheronne | Sherron | Hebrew | From Sharon, fertile plain |
| Sheryl | | French | Beloved |
| Shine | | American | |
| Shira | | Hebrew | My song |
| Shirley | | Anglo-Saxon | Willow farm |
| Shobhana | | Sanskrit | The beautiful one |
| Shona | | Irish | God is gracious |
| Shukuma | | African | Be thankful |
| Sian | | Irish | God is gracious |
| Sieglind | | German | Tender victory |
| Siena | Sienna | Italian | Italian city |
| Sierra | | Latin | From the mountains |
| Sigourney | | French | Daring king |
| Sigrid | | Scandinavian | Beautiful victory |
| Silje | | Scandinavian | Blind one |

| Name | Alternate spellings | Origin | Meaning |
|------|---------------------|--------|---------|
| Silke | | German | Blind one |
| Silvana | | Italian | From the forest |
| Silver | | Anglo-Saxon | Lustrous |
| Silvia | | Italian | From the forest |
| Simona | | Italian | The listener |
| Simone | | Hebrew | The listener |
| Sine | | Irish | God is gracious |
| Sinead | | Irish | God is gracious |
| Siobhan | | Irish | God is gracious |
| Siren | | Greek | Beautiful mythical women who lured sailors into the sea |
| Siri | | Scandinavian | Beautiful victory |
| Sisi | | African | Born on Sunday |
| Sissel | | Scandinavian | Blind one |
| Sissy | Cissy, Cicely | Anglo-Saxon | Blind one |
| Sita | | Sanskrit | The Hindu goddess of the harvest |
| Sitara | | Sanskrit | Morning star |
| Siti | | African | Lady |
| Siv | | Scandinavian | Bride |
| Sky | | Anglo-Saxon | Space above the ground |
| Skye | | Place name | Isle of Skye in Scotland |
| Snow | | Anglo-Saxon | Frozen water that falls from the sky |
| Snowflake | | Anglo-Saxon | Ice crystals that falls from the sky |
| Socorro | | Spanish | Helpful |
| Sofia | | Italian | Wisdom |
| Sofiya | | Russian | Wisdom |
| Solana | | Spanish | Sunlight and eastern breeze |

| Name | Alternate spellings | Origin | Meaning |
|------|---------------------|--------|---------|
| Soleil | | French | Sun |
| Song | | Anglo-Saxon | A piece of music |
| Sonia | Sonya | Anglo-Saxon | Wisdom |
| Sonora | | Celebrity child | (Alice and Sheryl Cooper) |
| Sonya | Sonia | Russian | Wisdom |
| Sophia | | Latin | Wisdom |
| Sophie | | French | Wisdom |
| Soraya | | Arabian | Weatlh, riches |
| Sorcha | | Irish | Shining |
| Sorrel | | English | Plant name |
| Spring | | Anglo-Saxon | Season before summer |
| Stacey | | Latin | Prosperous |
| Stasya | | Russian | Resurrection |
| Stefania | | Italian | Crown |
| Stefanie | Stef, Steffie | German | Crown |
| Stella | | Latin | A star |
| Stephanie | | Greek | Crown |
| Stevie | | Greek | A crown |
| Storm | | Anglo-Saxon | Thunder and lightening |
| Sue | | Hebrew | From Susan, lily |
| Sugar | | English | |
| Sujata | | Sanskrit | Of noble birth |
| Suki | | Japanese | Beloved |
| Sultana | | Arabic | Queen |
| Sumehra | | Arabic | Beautiful face |
| Summer | | Anglo-Saxon | The hottest season |
| Sunita | | Sanskrit | Of good conduct |
| Sunn | | Anglo-Saxon | Cheerful |
| Sunniva | | Anglo-Saxon | Gift of the sun |
| Sunset | | Anglo-Saxon | Time the sun disappears below the horizon |

| Name | Alternate spellings | Origin | Meaning |
|---|---|---|---|
| Sunshine | | Anglo-Saxon | Warmth and light of the sun |
| Susan | Sue, Susie, Suzie | Hebrew | A lily |
| Susanna | Sue, Susie, Suzie | Italian | A lily |
| Susannah | Sue, Susie, Suzie | Hebrew | A lily |
| Susanne | Sue, Susie, Suzie | French | A lily |
| Sveta | | Russian | Light |
| Svetlana | | Russian | Light |
| Swan | | English | White, graceful bird |
| Sweetie | | English | Cute |
| Sybil | | Greek | Mythical prophet |
| Sydney | | Place name | City in Australia |
| Sylvia | | Latin | From the woods |
| Sylvie | | French | From the woods |
| Symphony | | Latin | A piece of music |

| Name | Alternate spellings | Origin | Meaning |
|------|--------------------|--------|---------|
| **T** | | | |
| Tabita | | African | Graceful |
| Tabitha | Tabby | Greek | Gazelle |
| Taffeta | | American | Shiny material |
| Taffy | | Welsh | Beloved |
| Tahira | | Arabic | Virtuous |
| Tahirah | | Arabic | Virtuous |
| Talibah | | African | Intelligent |
| Tallara | | Australian | Rain |
| Tallulah | | Irish | Wealthy princess. Character in the play *Bugsy Malone* |
| Talwyn | | Cornish | Fair brow |
| Tamara | | Hebrew | A palm tree |
| Tamika | | African | Lively |
| Tamsin | Tammy | Anglo-Saxon | Benevolent |
| Tangelina | | Greek | Angel |
| Tanya | Tania | Russian | Derived from Roman family name Tatius |
| Tara | | Irish | Irish place name, seat of the high kings |
| Tarana | | Australian | A large waterhole |
| Tasha | Tash | Russian | Born at Christmas, from Natasha |
| Tate | Tait | Anglo-Saxon | Bringer of joy |
| Tathra | | Australian | Beautiful countryside |
| Tatum | | Anglo-Saxon | Bringer of joy |
| Tawia | | African | Born after twins |
| Taylor | | Anglo-Saxon | Cutter, person who makes clothes |

| Name | Alternate spellings | Origin | Meaning |
| --- | --- | --- | --- |
| Tegen | Teagan, Teagen | Welsh, Cornish | Pretty little thing |
| Tempest | | French | Tempestuous |
| Tennessee | | Place name | US state. First name of author Tennessee Williams |
| Teresa | Terry, Teri | Greek | Reaper |
| Terra | | Latin | Earth |
| Terri | Teri, Terry | Greek | Reaper |
| Tess | | Greek | Reaper |
| Tessa | | Greek | Reaper |
| Thada | | Greek | Thankful |
| Thalia | | Greek | Legendary muse of comedy |
| Thana | | Arabic | Thankful |
| Thara | | Arabic | Wealthy |
| Thelma | | Greek | A wish |
| Theodora | Theo | Greek | Gift of God |
| Thérèse | | French | Reaper |
| Theta | | Greek | Substantial |
| Thomasina | | Greek | A twin |
| Thora | | Scandinavian | From Norse god of thunder, Thor |
| Tia | | Spanish | Princess |
| Tiara | | Latin | Three-tiered crown |
| Tibby | | American | From Tabitha |
| Tierra | | Spanish | Earth |
| Tiffany | | Greek | Revelation of God |
| Tigerlily | | Celebrity child | (Paula Yates and Michael Hutchence) |
| Tilda | Tilde | Scandinavian | Mighty battle |
| Tilly | | German | From Matilda |
| Tina | | Latin | Little |

| Name | Alternate spellings | Origin | Meaning |
|------|---------------------|--------|---------|
| Tirranna | | Australian | Running water |
| Tisha | | African | Determined |
| Titania | | Greek | Great one. Fairy Queen in *A Midsummer Night's Dream* |
| Tiziana | | Italian | Great one |
| Toby | Tobie | Latin | God is good |
| Toffey | | American | From the sweet, toffee |
| Tony | Toni, Tonie | Latin | Worthy of praise |
| Topaz | | Sanskrit | Fire |
| Tora | | Scandinavian | Thunder |
| Tordis | | Scandinavian | Goddess, taken from Thor, Norse god of Thunder |
| Tori | Tory | Latin | From Victoria, winner |
| Tracey | Tracy | Gaelic | Fighter |
| Tree | | English | |
| Tricia | Trish, Trisha | Latin | Noble. From Patricia |
| Trina | | Greek | Pure. From Katrina |
| Trinity | | Latin | A trio |
| Trisha | Trish | Latin | From Patricia, noble |
| Trista | | Latin | Melancholy one |
| Trixie | Trixee | Latin | Pet name for Beatrix, voyager |
| Trotula | | Italian | From famous female doctor Trotula of Salemo |
| Trudy | Trude, Truda | German | Short for Gerturde or Ermentrude |

| Name | Alternate spellings | Origin | Meaning |
|------|--------------------|--------|---------|
| True | | American | |
| Truly | | American | |
| Tulia | | Spanish | Glorious |
| Tullia | | Italian | Heavy rain |
| Tully | | Irish | Powerful |
| Turin | | Place name | Italian town |
| Turua | | Pacific Islands | Beautiful |
| Twiggy | | English | Like a twig |
| Tyne | | Place name | English river |
| Tyra | | Scandinavian | Assertive |

| Name | Alternate spellings | Origin | Meaning |
|---|---|---|---|

# U

| Name | Alternate spellings | Origin | Meaning |
|---|---|---|---|
| Uda | | German | Prosperous |
| Udele | | Anglo-Saxon | Wealthy |
| Ula | | Welsh | Jewel of the sea |
| Ulani | | Pacific Islands | Happy |
| Ulima | | Arabic | Wise |
| Ulla | | Australian | A well |
| Ulrika | | Scandinavian | Wealthy and powerful |
| Uma | | Sanskrit | Light, peace |
| Umar | | Arabic | Flourishing |
| Umina | | Australian | Sleep |
| Unicorn | | English | Mythical horse-like creature with a horn |
| Unique | | English | One of a kind |
| Unity | | Latin | United |
| Urania | | Greek | Heavenly |
| Ursa | | Greek | Bear. Name of Ursa major and minor constellations |
| Ursula | | Hebrew | A bear |
| Usha | | Sanskrit | The dawn |
| Uta | | German | Rich |
| Utopia | | Greek | Perfect place |
| Uzima | | African | Vitality |
| Uzuri | | African | Beauty |

| Name | Alternate spellings | Origin | Meaning |
|------|--------------------|--------|---------|

# V

| Name | Alternate spellings | Origin | Meaning |
|------|--------------------|--------|---------|
| Vala | | Italian | Singled out |
| Valentina | | Italian | Healthy, right for marriage |
| Valentine | | Latin | Healthy, also the patron saint of lovers |
| Valérie | | French | Brave, courageous |
| Valeska | | Russian | Glorious ruler |
| Valletta | | | Place name: City in Malta |
| Valma | | Welsh | Mayflower |
| Vanessa | | Literary | Character in Jonathan Swift's *Gulliver's Travels* |
| Vanna | | Russian | God is gracious |
| Vasanti | | Sanskrit | Spring |
| Veda | | Sanskrit | Wisdom and knowledge |
| Vega | | Arabic | Falling. A star in the Lyra constellation |
| Velma | | American | Wilful, determined |
| Velvet | | English | Soft material |
| Venice | | Place name | Italian city |
| Ventura | | Spanish | The future |
| Venus | | Latin | Roman Goddess of beauty and love |
| Vera | | Latin | Truth |
| Verity | | Latin | Truth |
| Verona | | Place name | Italian city |
| Veronica | | Latin | True likeness |
| Véronique | | French | True likeness |
| Vesta | | Greek | Goddess of fire and the hearth |

| Name | Alternate Spellings | Origin | Meaning |
|---|---|---|---|
| Vic | | Latin | Victor, winner |
| Vicky | Vicki, Viki, Vikki | Latin | Victor, winner. Short for Victoria |
| Victoire | | French | Winner |
| Victoria | Vicky, Vicki, Viki, Vikki Tory, Vic | Latin | Victor, winner |
| Vida | | Latin | The beloved one |
| Vidya | | Sanskrit | Knowledge |
| Viki | Vicky, Vicki, Vikki | Latin | Victor, winner. From Victoria |
| Villette | | French | From the village |
| Vimala | | Sanskrit | Pure |
| Vina | | Spanish | Vineyard |
| Viola | | Italian | Violet |
| Violanda | | Italian | Violet |
| Violet | | Latin | A purple flower |
| Violetta | | Italian | Violet |
| Virdis | | Latin | Fresh, blooming |
| Virginia | | Latin | Chaste, pure |
| Virginie | Ginny | French | Pure, chaste |
| Virgo | | Latin | Virgin, maiden. Star sign and constellation |
| Vita | | Italian | Life |
| Vittoria | Vitoria | Italian, Spanish | Winner |
| Vivian | Vivienne | Latin | Lively |
| Viviana | | Italian | Lively |
| Vivienne | Vivian | French | Lively |
| Vladisalva | | Russian | To rule with glory |
| Vladmira | | Russian | To rule with greatness |
| Volante | | Latin | The flying one |
| Voletta | | French | Veiled |
| Vonda | | Russian | Of the Wend people |

| Name | Alternate spellings | Origin | Meaning |
|------|---------------------|--------|---------|

# W

| Name | Alternate spellings | Origin | Meaning |
|------|---------------------|--------|---------|
| Wahiba | | Arabic | Generous |
| Wahida | | Arabic | Unique |
| Walida | | Arabic | The newborn girl |
| Wallis | | Anglo-Saxon | Stranger |
| Wanda | | Anglo-Saxon | Young tree |
| Wangari | | African | Leopard |
| Wasima | | Arabic | Graceful, pretty |
| Wendelin | | German | Of the Wend people |
| Wendy | | Literary | *Peter Pan* by J. M. Barrie |
| Wenna | | Cornish | From St Wenn |
| Whitney | | Anglo-Saxon | From the white island |
| Widjan | | Arabic | Bliss |
| Wilda | | Anglo-Saxon | Wild |
| Wilhelmina | | German | Strong protector |
| Willa | | Anglo-Saxon | Determined |
| Willow | | Anglo-Saxon | From willow tree |
| Wilma | | German | Strong protector |
| Wilona | | Anglo-Saxon | Hoped for |
| Winifred | Winnie | Anglo-Saxon | Blessed peacemaker |
| Winky | | Literary | 'House elf' in *Harry Potter* series |
| Winna | | African | Friend |
| Winnie | | Anglo-Saxon | Blessed peacemaker |
| Winola | | German | Gracious friend |
| Winona | Winnie | American | American Indian for oldest daughter |
| Winsome | | Anglo-Saxon | Pleasant |
| Wren | | English | Small bird |
| Wylda | | German | Rebellious |

| Name | Alternate spellings | Origin | Meaning |
|------|---------------------|--------|---------|
| **X** | | | |
| Xaviera | | Italian, Spanish | Luminous |
| Xena | | Greek | Quest |
| Xiomara | | Spanish | Quest |
| Xuxa | | Spanish | Lily |
| Xylia | | Spanish | Woodland dweller |

| Name | Alternate spellings | Origin | Meaning |
|------|--------------------|--------|---------|

# Y

| Name | Alternate spellings | Origin | Meaning |
|------|--------------------|--------|---------|
| Yaa | | African | Born on Thursday |
| Yaffa | | Hebrew | Beautiful |
| Yakini | | African | Truth |
| Yancey | | American | From the term Yankee |
| Yani | | Australian | Peace |
| Yara | | Australian | A kind of bird |
| Yaromira | | Russian | A great spring |
| Yasmina | | Arabic | Jasmine flower |
| Yeira | | Hebrew | Light |
| Yelena | | Russian | Light of the sun |
| Yindi | | Australian | Sun |
| Yoko | | Japanese | Four, positive, side. Yoko Ono, John Lennon's wife |
| Yolanda | | Greek | Violet flower |
| Yomaris | | Spanish | I am the sun |
| Yoshiko | | Japanese | Good child |
| Yovela | | Hebrew | Rejoicing |
| Ysella | | Cornish | Modest |
| Ysobel | | Spanish | Consecrated to God |
| Yusra | | Arabic | Wealthy |
| Yvonne | | French | Young archer |

| Name | Alternate spellings | Origin | Meaning |
|------|---------------------|--------|---------|

# Z

| Name | Alternate spellings | Origin | Meaning |
|------|---------------------|--------|---------|
| Zabrina | | Anglo-Saxon | Noble maiden |
| Zada | Zaida | Arabic | Lucky |
| Zadie | | Arabic | From Zaida, prosperous |
| Zafiro | | Spanish | Sapphire |
| Zahara | | Arabic | A flower |
| Zahra | | Arabic | A flower |
| Zaina | | Arabic | Beautiful |
| Zakira | | Arabic | God has remembered |
| Zalika | | African | Well born |
| Zara | | Hebrew | The bright dawn |
| Zarifa | | Arabic | Graceful |
| Zawadi | | African | Gift |
| Zebada | | Hebrew | The Lord's gift |
| Zelda | | Anglo-Saxon | Companion |
| Zelia | | Greek | Zealous, dutiful |
| Zelma | | Literary | Beautiful appearance |
| Zena | | Greek | Hospitable |
| Zenith | | Arabic | The highest point |
| Zennor | | Place name | Cornish village |
| Zera | | Greek | Seeds |
| Zhenya | | Russian | Of good birth |
| Zia | | Arabic | Splendour |
| Zina | | Russian | Shining or sky |
| Zinaida | | Russian | Shining or sky |
| Zinovia | | Russian | Life of Zeus |
| Ziona | | Hebrew | A sign |
| Zita | | Latin | Patron saint of domestic servants |
| Ziva | | Hebrew | Brightness |
| Zoë | | Greek | Life |

| Name | Alternate spellings | Origin | Meaning |
|------|--------------------|--------|---------|
| Zohara | | Hebrew | The bright child |
| Zohra | | Arabic | Blossoming |
| Zola | | Latin | Earth |
| Zora | | Latin | The dawn |
| Zulema | | Arabic | Peace |
| Zuwina | | African | Good |

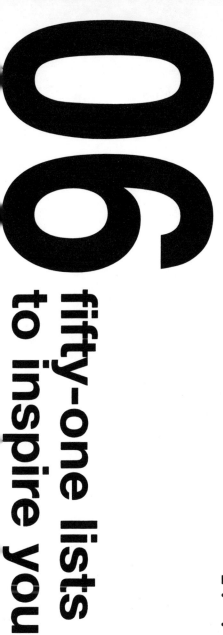

# 06

# fifty-one lists to inspire you

**In this chapter you will learn:**
- favourite names from particular origins
- great names to suit different occupations and lifestyles
- names inspired by celebrities, songs, myth and literature.

# 1. Latin names

## Boys

Adrian
Alban
Albion
Albus
Amadeus
Anthony
Aurelius
Ben
Benedict
Benjamin
Bennet
Bennett
Benson
Blaise
Calvin
Cassius
Cecil
Chester
Christian
Cicero
Clarence
Clark
Claude
Clement
Cornelius
Crispin
Cupid
Dean
Deo
Dexter
Dominic
Draco
Emil
Errol
Fabian

Faustus
Felix
Festus
Fidel
Figaro
Filius
Firenze
Francis
Frankie
Gilderoy
Guy
Hilary
Horace
Horatio
Jet
Jove
Judd
Jules
Julius
Justin
Justus
Krispin
Lacy
Larry
Laurence
Laurie
Lawrence
Leo
Léon
Lionel
Lorimer
Lucian
Lucius
Ludo
Marc

Marcus
Mark
Martin
Maurice
Mayer
Miles
Morris
Mundungus
Myles
Mylo
Nemo
Nero
Nigel
Nimrod
Octavius
Oliver
Orsen
Paddy
Pascal
Pat
Patrick
Paul
Peregrine
Phineas
Placido
Primo
Prince
Quentin
Quincy
Rebel
Remus
Rex
Romeo
Rufus
Salazar

Sebastian
Severus
Silas
Silvester
Sirius
Sol
Sylvester
Tarquin
Terence
Terry
Tivon
Tobias
Tobie
Toby
Todd
Tony
Torrence
Trent
Turner
Urban
Usher
Valentine
Vernon
Vic
Victor
Vidal
Vince
Vincent
Vinnie
Virgil
Voldemort

# Girls

| | |
|---|---|
| Adriana | Cybill |
| Alida | Dahlia |
| Amity | Delphine |
| Anabelle | Delphinium |
| Antonia | Demi |
| April | Diana |
| Arabella | Dinah |
| Aria | Drusilla |
| Ariana | Dulcie |
| Aurelia | Erma |
| Barbara | Estelle |
| Beatrice | Felicia |
| Begonia | Felicity |
| Bellatrix | Felita |
| Benedicta | Fleur |
| Brittany | Flora |
| Camelia | Florence |
| Camilla | Florida |
| Camille | Frances |
| Candice | Frankie |
| Carissa | Gardenia |
| Carmel | Gazelle |
| Cassia | Gemma |
| Cecilia | Gill |
| Celeste | Gillian |
| Charity | Ginny |
| Charmaine | Gloria |
| Chastity | Grace |
| Chris | Hilary |
| Christina | Honour |
| Claire | Hyacinth |
| Clarice | Imogen |
| Clarissa | Irma |
| Claudia | Jill |
| Connie | Jillian |
| Coral | Joquil |
| Cornelia | Joy |
| Crisanta | Joyce |

Jules
Julia
Julie
Justine
Lara
Latisha
Laura
Laurel
Lauren
Lavinia
Leandra
Lenita
Leonie
Letitia
Liberty
Lori
Lotus
Lucilla
Lucinda
Lucy
Luna
Maia
Mara
Marcella
Marcia
Margeurite
Maria
Marigold
Marina
Marsha
Martine
Mary
Maxine
Meryl
Minerva
Mirabelle
Miranda
Miriam

Monica
Myra
Nat
Natalie
Nola
Noreen
Nydia
Octavia
Olivia
Pansy
Pat
Patricia
Patsy
Paula
Pax
Pomona
Porsche
Portia
Primrose
Prudence
Prunella
Questa
Quinella
Quita
Rain
Regina
Rene
Renite
Romilly
Rosa
Rosalia
Rosalie
Rosalind
Rosalyn
Rosamond
Rose
Rosemary
Rosie

Rowena
Ruby
Sabina
Sabine
Serena
Serenity
Sheila
Sierra
Sophia
Stacey
Stella
Sylvia
Symphony
Terra
Tina
Toby
Tony
Tori
Tricia
Trinity
Trisha

Trista
Unity
Valentine
Venus
Vera
Verity
Veronica
Vic
Vicky
Victoria
Vida
Viki
Violet
Virdis
Virginia
Vivian
Volante
Zita
Zola
Zora

# 2. Greek names

## Boys

Achilles
Adonis
Ajax
Alex
Alexander
Alexis
Ambrose
Anatole
Andrew
Apollo
Arcadio
Archimedes
Argus
Arion
Aristo
Artemas
Athan
Balthasar
Balthazar
Barnabas
Barnaby
Basil
Christopher
Cosmo
Cyril
Damien
Darien
Darius
Deacon
Dedalus
Dennis
Drew
Erasmus
Eros
Eugene
Eustace

Galen
Gene
George
Giles
Gregory
Griffin
Hagrid
Hector
Hercules
Hermes
Jason
Jerome
Kit
Kristopher
Leander
Linus
Luke
Lysander
Magnus
Neo
Nestor
Nicholas
Nike
Ocean
Otis
Palladin
Par
Paris
Peter
Philip
Philo
Phoenix
Piers
Pip
Rubeus
Sandy

Stacey
Stavros
Stelios
Stephen
Steven
Thaddeus
Theo
Theodore
Theron
Thomas
Tim
Timothy

Titan
Tom
Tommy
Tomo
Ulysses
Xander
Xanthus
Xeno
Yannis
Zander
Zeth
Zeus

## Girls

Adelpha
Agape
Agatha
Agnes
Alanis
Alessandra
Alethea
Alex
Alexandra
Alexis
Alice
Alicia
Alison
Alyssa
Amara
Amaryllis
Aminta
Andrea
Andy
Angela
Angelica
Aphrodite
Araminta
Aretha
Asia
Asta
Astra
Athena
Aura
Ava
Azalea
Berenice
Beryl
Bryony
Calla
Callidora
Callista
Calypso

Cassandra
Catherine
Celene
Celina
Celine
Charis
Charisma
Charissa
Chloe
Chrysilla
Cilla
Cindy
Cleo
Clio
Cora
Cosima
Crystal
Cynthia
Damara
Daphne
Daria
Deianeira
Dell
Della
Denise
Dido
Dione
Dora
Dorian
Doris
Dorothy
Drew
Ebony
Echo
Effie
Elaine
Eleanor
Electra

Ellie
Eudora
Eunice
Eustacia
Evangelia
Gaea
Gaia
Georgia
Georgina
Gina
Greer
Harmony
Helen
Hermione
Hypatia
Ianthe
Iola
Iolanthe
Irene
Iris
Isadora
Jacaranda
Jacinda
Kara
Karen
Karis
Karissa
Kate
Katharine
Kit
Krysanthe
Kyra
Leda
Leora
Lesbia
Lexie
Lissa
Lydia
Lyra

Lysander
Lysandra
Maggie
Margaret
Melanie
Melina
Melinda
Melissa
Melody
Myrtle
Narcissa
Nereida
Nerissa
Neroli
Nicky
Nicola
Nike
Nikita
Nymphadora
Nyx
Odessa
Oleander
Ophelia
Oprah
Pamela
Pandora
Paris
Pelagia
Penelope
Penny
Peta
Philippa
Philly
Philomena
Phoebe
Phoenix
Phyliss
Phyllida
Pippa

Psyche
Reenie
Rhea
Rhoda
Samantha
Sandrea
Sandy
Sapphire
Selena
Selene
Stephanie
Stevie
Sybil
Tabitha
Tangelina
Teresa
Terri
Tess
Tessa

Thada
Thalia
Thelma
Theodora
Theta
Thomasina
Tiffany
Titania
Trina
Urania
Vesta
Xena
Yolanda
Zelia
Zena
Zera
Zoe

# 3. Anglo-Saxon names

## Boys

Ainsley
Albert
Alden
Aldon
Aldwin
Alfie
Alfred
Algar
Alger
Alvin
Alwyn
Armstrong
Ash
Ashley
Aston
Aubrey
Auden
Avery
Barclay
Barney
Baron
Bartemius
Bartholomew
Barton
Baxter
Beethoven
Bernard
Bertram
Bill
Billy
Blake
Bobby
Bond
Bosley
Bradford
Brandon

Branson
Brock
Bron
Bronson
Bronze
Brook
Brown
Bud
Buddy
Byron
Carrington
Chad
Chandler
Chopin
Cirrus
Cliff
Clifford
Clint
Clinton
Clive
Cloud
Cody
Colby
Cooper
Courtney
Curtis
Cuthbert
Cyclone
Darren
Dell
Denby
Denton
Digby
Dudley
Durwin
Durwyn

Dustin
Earl
Eddison
Edgar
Edmund
Edward
Edwin
Eldon
Eldrid
Eldwyn
Elmer
Elton
Elvis
Emmet
Eric
Esmond
Evelyn
Farley
Ferdinand
Fire
Flame
Floyd
Foley
Ford
Forest
Fowler
Frank
Franklin
Fred
Frederick
Freeman
Geoff
Geoffrey
Gerald
Gerard
Gladwyn

Godric
Gordon
Graham
Guillaume
Hail
Hamilton
Harrison
Harry
Hartley
Hayward
Heath
Henderson
Henry
Hilton
Holden
Holder
Hugh
Hurricane
Huxley
Ice
Ingram
Irwin
Ivor
Jack
Jackson
Jagger
Jaimie
James
Jarvis
Jasper
Jeffrey
Jeremy
Jevon
Jim
Jools
Kendall

| | |
|---|---|
| Kim | Onslow |
| King | Orme |
| Kinglsey | Orvin |
| Kipp | Orvyn |
| Kirby | Osborne |
| Knox | Osburt |
| Lance | Osgood |
| Lane | Osmond |
| Langley | Oswald |
| Leaf | Palmer |
| Lee | Parker |
| Leighton | Patton |
| Lester | Paxton |
| Lewis | Pearson |
| Linford | Piper |
| Lyman | Pollock |
| Lyndon | Presley |
| Lindsey | Preston |
| Mallory | Radley |
| Manfred | Ralph |
| Marley | Ramsey |
| Marvin | Randolf |
| Maxwell | Randolph |
| Maynard | Randy |
| Melbourne | Red |
| Merton | Reeve |
| Milburn | Richard |
| Morrissey | Ridgley |
| Morton | Ripple |
| Ned | Robert |
| Nellie | Robin |
| Newton | Robson |
| Nixon | Rochester |
| Norman | Rock |
| Norton | Rocky |
| Norward | Roderick |
| Oakley | Roland |
| Odin | Rowan |
| Ogden | Royce |

Royston
Rudd
Russell
Rusty
Rutledge
Sanders
Sanford
Saxon
Scott
Selwin
Selwyn
Shamrock
Shandy
Shelby
Sheldon
Shelley
Sherwin
Sherwyn
Shipley
Sinclair
Sinjon
Slade
Smith
Smokey
Stanley
Starr
Stewart
Storm
Stuart
Sumner

Tate
Taylor
Ted
Thane
Theobald
Tor
Travis
Truman
Tucker
Tyler
Umber
Vance
Vere
Wallace
Wallis
Walter
Warren
Wayne
Webster
Wilbur
Wilfred
Willis
Wilson
Winston
Woodrow
Woody
Worth
Wycliff
Wynne
Yardley

# Girls

Acorn
Alberta
Apple
Ash
Ashley
Audrey
Autumn
Beatrix
Berry
Billie
Blossom
Bluebell
Blythe
Bobby
Bonnie
Bramble
Brook
Carole
Chelsea
Cirrus
Cloud
Clover
Crystal
Daisy
Dandelion
Darcy
Dawn
Dusk
Eartha
Edith
Edwina
Elvina
Elwyn
Elysia
Ethel
Etta
Fay
Fen

Fern
Godiva
Goldie
Halle
Hayley
Hazel
Heather
Helga
Hester
Holly
Ivy
Jada
Jade
Joan
Kendra
Kim
Kimberley
Leaf
Lee
Leigh
Lilac
Lillian
Lily
Linn
Lois
Loveday
Lunar
Lyn
Lyndsey
Lynn
Madison
Madonna
Magenta
Maisie
Marian
Martha
Matilda
Maud

Mildred
Milly
Moon
Nelly
Norma
Ocean
Olive
Ora
Peace
Peach
Pearl
Pebbles
Peggy
Petal
Petula
Petunia
Pink
Piper
Pixie
Plum
Polly
Poppy
Presley
Providence
Queenie
Quenna
Radella
Rae
Raindrop
Ramona
Randi
Rexanne
Ripple
Robin
Scarlet
Shelby
Shelley
Shirley

Silver
Sissy
Sky
Snow
Snowflake
Song
Spring
Storm
Summer
Sunn
Sunniva
Sunset
Sunshine
Tamsin
Tate
Tatum
Taylor
Udele
Wallis
Wanda
Whitney
Wilda
Willa
Willow
Wilona
Winifred
Winnie
Winsome
Zabrina
Zelda

# 4. Irish names

## Boys

Aidan
Alan
Alister
Allan
Bairrie
Barry
Blaine
Blair
Blayney
Brendan
Brian
Broderick
Brody
Bryan
Cal
Callum
Carbry
Casey
Cassidy
Clancy
Codie
Cody
Coleman
Colin
Colm
Conan
Conn
Conor
Corey
Cormac
Daley
Darcy
Daric
Darragh
Darrick

Dary
Declan
Delaney
Dempsey
Dermot
Desmond
Devin
Devlyn
Diarmaid
Donovan
Doyle
Drake
Dwayne
Dwyer
Eamon
Erin
Farrell
Fearghal
Ferghus
Fergus
Ferguson
Finbar
Findlay
Finlay
Finn
Finnegan
Flannagan
Flynn
Gallagher
Guthne
Haley
Harvey
Hurley
Innis
Jackie

Kane
Kasey
Keagan
Kean
Keanan
Kearney

Keefe
Keegan
Keenan
Kelly
Kelvin
Ken
Kendrick
Kennedy
Kenneth
Kevin
Kieran
Lennon
Liam
Logan
Maclain
Mahoney
Malone
Melvin
Monroe
Neal
Niall
Nolan
Nyle
Orran
Quinn
Reagan
Regan
Rehgan
Riley

Roark
Roary
Ronan
Rorke
Ryan
Scanlan
Seamus
Sean
Shaine
Shamus
Shane
Shannon
Shaun
Shauny
Shayne
Sullivan
Sweeney
Tiernan
Trevor
Troy
Tuily
Tyrone

# Girls

Adan
Aidan
Aine
Aiofe
Aislin
Aithne
Alana
Alannah
Alayna
Blaine
Bridget
Brighid
Brigid
Caitlin
Caoimhe
Casey
Colleen
Corey
Dana
Deirdre
Dervla
Doherty
Eileen
Ena
Erin
Grainne
Granya
Ina
Kacie
Kaitline
Keana
Keely
Kelly
Kerry
Kiera
Kyle
Maeve
Maire

Maureen
Megan
Moira
Molly
Mona
Morna
Moyna
Nancy
Nia
Niamh
Orla
Roisin
Ros
Sadhbh [pr: syve]
Sean
Shane
Shannon
Shauny
Shavon
Shea
Shona
Sian
Sine
Sinead
Siobhan
Sorcha
Tallulah
Tara
Tully

# 5. Welsh names

## Boys

Alun
Anwell
Anwyl
Arlin
Arthur
Artie
Bardan
Bevan
Boden
Bowden
Bowen
Bowie
Bradan
Bram
Bran
Brennan
Brent
Bret
Bryce
Bryn
Cadan
Cadwur
Cai
Caio
Caradoc
Caradwg
Cary
Ciaran
Daffyd
Dai
Davin
Dillan
Dillon
Dylan
Emrys

Evan
Gareth
Gary
Gavin
Gawain
Gethin
Glyn
Gowan
Ioan
Kay
Keith
Kent
Kirwyn
Lincoln
Llewelyn
Lloyd
Lynn
Maddox
Meredith
Merlin
Newlin
Owen
Reece
Rhett
Rhys
Romney
Taliesin
Tristan
Tristram
Trystan
Vaughn
Yale

## Girls

| | |
|---|---|
| Arianwyn | Gwynedd |
| Arwyn | Gwyneth |
| Blodeyn | Jennifer |
| Blodwedd | Jenny |
| Brangwen | Kay |
| Bronagh | Kiera |
| Bronwen | Llewella |
| Bryn | Lowri |
| Cal | Lynette |
| Caron | Meredith |
| Carwyn | Morwenna |
| Cary | Nerys |
| Carys | Olwen |
| Celyn | Orin |
| Ceri | Rhianna |
| Ceridwen | Rhiannon |
| Cerys | Rhonwen |
| Ciara | Rosslyn |
| Crystin | Sabrina |
| Delwyn | Taffy |
| Dilwen | Tegen |
| Dilys | Ula |
| Eira | Valma |
| Enid | |
| Ffion | |
| Fiona | |
| Gladys | |
| Glenda | |
| Glenys | |
| Glynis | |
| Guinevere | |
| Gwen | |
| Gwendolin | |
| Gweneth | |
| Gweniver | |
| Gwyn | |

# 6. Scottish names

## Boys

Alan
Alasdair
Alistair
Anghus
Archie
Boyd
Brian
Bryan
Cal
Callum
Cam
Cameron
Campbell
Clyde
Coleman
Conall
Craig
Dalziel
Darragh
Domhnall
Donal
Donald
Dougal
Douglas
Duncan
Dunmor
Euan
Ewan
Fife
Findlay
Finlay
Gillespie
Gilroy
Glen
Graeme
Grant
Hamish
Harvey
Iain

Ian
Jackie
Jock
Kyle
Leith
Lennox
Lesley
Lyle
Mac
Malcolm
McCartney
Morgan
Mungo
Murdoch
Murray
Neil
Quigley
Quinlan
Reid
Ronald
Rooney
Ross
Skelly

## Girls

Aileen
Ailsa
Arlene
Elspeth
Glen
Isa
Isla
Janet
Kathleen
Kirstin
Kirsty
Lesley
Netta
Paisley

# 7. Cornish names

## Boys

Arthur
Artie
Benesek
Cador
Caradoc
Denzel
Gwithyen
Jacca
Jago
Jowan
Kevern
Lewyth
Mawgan
Piran
Rewan
Tristan
Trystan
Uther

## Girls

Bennath
Blejan
Borra
Bronnen
Bryluen
Dellen
Demelza
Ebrel
Enor
Guinevere
Gwaynten
Gwiryon
Gwynder
Jenna
Kerensa
Kerra
Lamorna
Lowenna
Morenwyn
Morwenna
Rosenwyn
Senara
Talwyn
Wenna
Ysella

# 8. German names

## Boys

Abelard
Adelbert
Adolf
Amory
Anselm
Archibald
Arnold
Bernhard
Berthold
Bruno
Carl
Christhard
Claus
Colbert
Conrad
Dieter
Ebbo
Ernst
Evert
Franz
Frederik
Friedrich
Fritz
Fulbright
Godfrey
Gunther
Hansel
Heinrich
Heinz
Helmut
Herbert
Hermann
Howe
Hubert

Hugo
Humbert
Humphrey
Ingelbert
Karl
Karsten
Keane
Konrad
Kurt
Ludwig
Luther
Lyulf
Napolean
Norbert
Otto
Robert
Roger
Roland
Rolf
Rory
Rudi
Rudolf
Rupert
Siegfried
Siegmund
Stefan
Ulrich
Volker
Waldo
Wendel
Wilhelm
Willard
Wolf
Wolfgang

## Girls

Ada
Adelheide
Aleida
Berta
Bertha
Christa
Dietlind
Ebba
Edda
Elke
Elsa
Emil
Emily
Emma
Emmeline
Ermentrude
Frieda
Gertrude
Hedwig
Heidi
Hilda
Ilse
Katharina
Liese

Lorelei
Lotte
Luise
Lulu
Magda
Magdalene
Marlene
Mina
Mitzi
Romy
Rudy
Sieglind
Silke
Stefanie
Tilly
Trudy
Uda
Uta
Wendelin
Wilhelmina
Wilma
Winola
Wylda

# 9. Scandinavian names

## Boys

| | |
|---|---|
| Ake | Knut |
| Amund | Kristian |
| Anders | Morten |
| Ari | Niels |
| Arvid | Niklaus |
| Asmund | Nordin |
| Axel | Ola |
| Bjorn | Olaf |
| Broder | Oman |
| Caspar | Pal |
| Erik | Pitney |
| Erland | Quimby |
| Finn | Ragnar |
| Frode | Roald |
| Gunne | Rothwell |
| Gustav | Rune |
| Halvard | Skip |
| Harald | Sondre |
| Havard | Soren |
| Ivar | Sven |
| Johanne | Sverre |
| Kaspar | Tor |
| Kelsey | Ulrik |

# Girls

Annika
Asa
Asta
Astrid
Barbro
Birgit
Bo
Britt
Christer
Dagmar
Dagna
Disa
Erika
Freja
Gerd
Gudrun
Helga
Hertha
Hulda
Ikea
Ingrid
Jensine
Kaisa
Karita
Katarina
Katharina
Kirsten
Kristen
Liv
Lovisa
Marna
Merete
Mia
Nanna
Ola
Quinby
Rakel
Rona
Runa
Saga
Saskia
Sassa
Sigrid
Silje
Siri
Sissel
Siv
Thora
Tilda
Tora
Tordis
Tyra
Ulrika

# 10. Sanskrit names

## Boys

| | |
|---|---|
| Ambar | Mani |
| Amrit | Mohan |
| Anand | Mohinder |
| Anil | Nanda |
| Arjun | Narayan |
| Arun | Narendra |
| Ashok | Prakash |
| Bharat | Prasad |
| Bhima | Prem |
| Chandan | Raj |
| Chandra | Rajendra |
| Deepak | Rajiv |
| Dev | Ramesh |
| Devdan | Ranjit |
| Dinesh | Ravi |
| Ganesh | Sanjay |
| Gautama | Sankara |
| Ghandi | Shankar |
| Gopal | Sharma |
| Govinda | Sher |
| Hari | Shiva |
| Indra | Siddartha |
| Jagdish | Suman |
| Jitender | Suresh |
| Jyotis | Surya |
| Kama | Taj |
| Karan | Tarun |
| Kiran | Ushnisha |
| Krishna | Vamana |
| Kumar | Varuna |
| Lai | Vasudeva |
| Lakshman | Vidya |
| Ljluka | Vijay |
| Mahatma | Vimal |
| Mahendra | Vishnu |
| Mahesh | Wassily |

## Girls

| | |
|---|---|
| Ambar | Mohana |
| Amrita | Nagini |
| Ananda | Nalini |
| Anila | Opal |
| Aruna | Padma |
| Asha | Parminder |
| Avara | Parvati |
| Bala | Prema |
| Chandani | Priya |
| Chandi | Purnima |
| Chandra | Radha |
| Devika | Rajani |
| Dharma | Rani |
| Durga | Rati |
| Gita | Rohana |
| Indira | Rukmini |
| Jalini | Sanila |
| Jama | Sarisha |
| Jarita | Saroja |
| Jaya | Shakti |
| Jyoti | Shakuntala |
| Kali | Shamra |
| Kalinda | Shanti |
| Kalpana | Sharmila |
| Kalyani | Sheela |
| Kama | Sher |
| Kamala | Shobhana |
| Kanti | Sita |
| Kumari | Sitara |
| Lakshmi | Sujata |
| Lalita | Sunita |
| Leela | Topaz |
| Madhuri | Uma |
| Malati | Usha |
| Mani | Vasanti |
| Manjusha | Veda |
| Meena | Vidya |
| | Vimala |

# 11. Arabic names

## Boys

Abbas
Abdel
Abdullah
Abir
Adil
Adnan
Ahmed
Akbar
Akeem
Akil
Akram
Aladdin
Ali
Alim
Amal
Amin
Amir
Ansari
Anwar
Ashraf
Asim
Aswad
Azim
Aziz
Bashir
Basim
Bilal
Cemal
Emir
Fadil
Faisal
Farid
Farook
Faysal
Feroz

Ferran
Firdos
Gamal
Ghassan
Ginton
Habib
Hadi
Hafiz
Hakim
Hamal
Hamid
Hani
Hasim
Hassan
Hussain
Imam
Jabir
Jaleel
Jalil
Jamal
Kadin
Kadir
Kalid
Kalil
Kamal
Kamil
Karim
Kasim
Kateb
Kedar
Kemal
Khalid
Khalif
Khalil
Latif

Mahmood
Mahomet
Majid
Malik
Mansoor
Masud
Mohammed
Mubarak
Muhammad
Mukhtar
Nabil
Nadir
Nasir
Nassir
Nuri
Omar
Osman
Qabil
Qadir
Qasim
Quasim
Rafi
Rafiq
Rahman
Rashid
Rauf
Sabir
Sadik
Salah
Salim
Salman
Sarni
Sayed
Seif
Selim
Seyed
Shafiq
Shakar
Shakir

Sharif
Shunnar
Tahir
Tamir
Tariq
Umar
Usman
Wahib
Walid
Wasim
Xerxes
Yasir
Yazid
Zade
Zafar
Zahir
Zaki
Zia

## Girls

Aaliyah
Abia
Abir
Adar
Adara
Adiba
Adila
Adiva
Afraima
Aiesha
Ain
Aisha
Akila
Akilah
Ali
Alima
Aliya
Aliyah
Almira

Alzena
Amala
Amani
Amber
Ambra
Ameerah

Amina
Amira
Anan
Anisa
Annissa
Atifa
Atiya
Aziza
Azra
Barakah
Basimah
Bibi
Cala
Cantara
Elma
Esther
Fadila
Faiza
Farah
Farida
Fatima
Fatin
Ghada
Habiba
Hadya
Haifa
Hana
Hasna
Hayfa
Helima
Imam
Iman
Isra

Israt
Jala
Jalila
Jamal
Jamelia
Jamila
Jamilah
Janan
Janna
Jarnila
Jasmine
Jehan
Jira
Kadira
Kaela
Kalila
Kamil
Kamilah
Karida
Karima
Kebira
Khalida
Latifa
Leila
Lila
Lilith
Lina
Lyla
Mahala
Malak
Malika
Matana
Maysa
Medina
Melek
Muna
Munira
Muriel
Myiesha

Nabila
Nada
Nadira
Nafeeza
Nawal
Nazirah
Nimah
Noor
Noya
Oma
Qadira
Qamra
Rabi
Raja
Rana
Rashida
Roxanna
Roxanne
Roxy
Sabah
Sabira
Saffron
Safia
Sahar
Sahara
Saida
Sakinah
Salima
Salimah
Salwa
Samirah
Samma
Sana
Saree
Sawsan
Shahira
Shakira
Sultana
Sumehra

Tahira
Tahirah
Thana
Thara
Tulin
Ulima
Umar
Vega
Wahiba
Wahida
Walida
Wasima
Widjan
Yasmina
Yusra
Zada
Zadie
Zahara
Zahra
Zaina
Zakira
Zarifa
Zenith
Zia
Zohra
Zulema

# 12. French names

## Boys

| | |
|---|---|
| Aimé | Étienne |
| Alain | Farquar |
| Alec | Fran |
| Aleron | François |
| Alexandre | Fraser |
| Amaury | Frasier |
| Ancel | Frédéric |
| André | Gérard |
| Antoine | Germain |
| Anton | Gervaise |
| Armand | Grégoire |
| Armani | Henri |
| Arnaud | Honoré |
| Auguste | Jacques |
| Augustin | Jean |
| Bailey | Jermaine |
| Beau | Julian |
| Beaumont | Laurent |
| Benoît | Leroy |
| Bertrand | Louis |
| Camilo | Luc |
| Charles | Lucas |
| Charlie | Macy |
| Chase | Marcel |
| Chevalier | Marmion |
| Christophe | Matthieu |
| Darell | Melville |
| Darryl | Merrill |
| Dartagnan | Michel |
| Didier | Moore |
| Diggory | Morell |
| Dominique | Nicolas |
| Donatien | Noe |
| Édouard | Noël |
| Émile | Norville |
| Esme | Olivier |

Percival
Percy
Philippe
Pierre
Ray
Raymond
Rémy
René
Roy
Saville
Serge
Seymore
Sidney
Sorrel
Stéphane
Talbot
Théodore
Théophile
Thierry
Vivian
Xavier
Yves
Zacharie

## Girls

Adèle
Adrienne
Aerien
Agathe
Aimée
Alea
Alize
Amalie
Amarante
Amélie
Amerique
Anaïs
Anastasie
Andrée

Ange
Anjanette
Anouk
Antoinette
Astrid
Aurélie
Aurore
Avril
Babette
Bailey
Bella
Belle
Bernadette
Bijou
Bonte
Brie
Brier
Brigitte
Capucine
Caresse
Caron
Cécile
Chanel
Chanelle
Chantal
Chante
Charlene
Charlize
Charlotte
Chaton
Cheryl
Christelle
Christiane
Christine
Claudette
Claudine
Clémence
Colette
Corinne

Courtney
Danielle
Darlene

Deja
Delice
Desiree
Diamanta
Diane
Dior
Dominique
Dore
Doreen
Dori
Dorothée
Élise
Elle
Elodie
Élodie
Eloise
Émilie
Emmanuelle
Fleurette
Fossetta
Françoise
Frédérique
Gabrielle
Garland
Gay
Geneva
Geneviève
Germaine
Harriette
Hélène
Henriette
Hortense
Inès
Isabelle
Jacqueline
Jacquetta

Jamais
Janelle
Jean
Jeanne
Jeannine
Jolie
Josette
Juillet
Juliette
Jumelle
Laure
Leala
Linette
Lorraine
Louise
Mabel
Mai
Malory
Manon
Marcelle
Mardi
Margaux
Margot
Marianne
Marie
Marine
Marjorie
Marvelle
Maryse
Mathilde
Merise
Michèle
Mignon
Monique
Musique
Nanette
Nathalie
Nettie
Nicole

Noelle
Océane
Odette
Olivie
Orene
Page
Pascale
Paulette
Pauline
Philippine
Raissa
Renée
Roche
Rochelle
Royale
Safran
Saison
Satine

Shance
Sheryl
Sigourney
Soleil
Sophie
Susanne
Sylvie
Tempest
Thérèse
Valérie
Véronique
Victoire
Villette
Virginie
Vivienne
Voletta
Yvonne

# 13. Italian names

## Boys

Abbondanzio
Abbondio
Abelardo
Abele
Abelino
Abramo
Addolorata
Achille
Agatino
Adalfredo
Adalgisio
Adalrico
Adriano
Alarico
Alberico
Alberto
Aldo
Alessio
Alfonsino
Alfredo
Alvaro
Amalio
Amaranto
Amerigo
Angelo
Antonio
Ariosto
Armando
Basso
Benito
Bernardo
Bertoldo
Biagio
Bonifacio
Boris
Bruno

Caio
Camillo
Carisio
Carlo
Cassio
Cataldo
Celio
Cesare
Cherubino
Cino
Cipriano
Claudio
Concordio
Cornelio
Cosimo
Costanzo
Cristiano
Dante
Dario
Demetrio
Diego
Dimitri
Dino
Domenico
Durante
Eberardo
Edilio
Edmondo
Eduardo
Elia
Eliano
Eligio
Emanuele
Emidio
Emilio
Ennio

| | |
|---|---|
| Enrico | Guido |
| Erizo | Lamberto |
| Ercole | Landro |
| Eric | Leo |
| Eros | Leonardo |
| Ezio | Leone |
| Fabio | Leopoldo |
| Fabrizio | Liberio |
| Fausto | Libero |
| Federico | Lisandro |
| Ferdinando | Lorenzo |
| Ferruccio | Luca |
| Fidenzio | Luciano |
| Filiberto | Lucio |
| Filippo | Lucius |
| Fiorello | Luigi |
| Fiorenzo | Manuel |
| Firenze | Marcello |
| Flavio | Marco |
| Fosco | Mariano |
| Francesco | Mario |
| Franco | Martino |
| Furio | Massimo |
| Gabriele | Michelangelo |
| Galileo | Muzio |
| Gandolfo | Narciso |
| Gaspare | Nereo |
| Gennaro | Nino |
| Geraldo | Olindo |
| Geronimo | Olivero |
| Giancarlo | Omero |
| Gianetto | Oreste |
| Gianfranco | Orlando |
| Gianni | Oronzo |
| Gildo | Orso |
| Gino | Ortensio |
| Giorgio | Oscar |
| Giovanni | Ottone |
| Guiseppe | Ovidio |
| Gregorio | Paciano |

Palmiro
Paolo
Piero
Pietro

Pio
Placido
Prospero
Raimondo
Ramiro
Raul
Renato
Ricardo
Rinaldo
Roberto
Rocco
Rodolfo
Rodrigo
Roland
Rolando
Romano
Romeo
Romolo
Rufino
Salvatore
Salvo
Samuele
Sante
Santo
Saverio
Serafino
Sergio
Severo
Silvano
Silvestro
Silvio
Siro
Stefano
Terenzio
Tito

Tommaso
Umberto
Uriele
Valentino
Valerio
Vincenzo
Vitale
Vito
Vittore

## Girls

Abela
Abelina
Ada
Adalberta
Adalgisa
Adelaide
Adelfina
Adelia
Adelinda
Adriana
Alberta
Albertina
Albina
Alda
Alfonsina
Alfreda
Alfredina
Alida
Alma
Aloisia
Alvisa
Amalia
Ambretta
Angelica
Angelina
Anita
Anna
Anna Maria

| | |
|---|---|
| Annabella | Cornelia |
| Annabel | Crispina |
| Antonella | Cristiano |
| Antonietta | Cristina |
| Arabella | Dalia |
| Arianna | Dalila |
| Artemisia | Damiana |
| Aurelia | Daniela |
| Aurora | Daphne |
| Barbara | Daria |
| Batilda | Deborah |
| Beatrice | Delfina |
| Belinda | Delinda |
| Berenice | Delmina |
| Berta | Demetria |
| Bianca | Dina |
| Bibiana | Domenica |
| Brigida | Donatella |
| Bruna | Dorotea |
| Camelia | Elda |
| Camilla | Elena |
| Candida | Eleonora |
| Carla | Eliana |
| Carmela | Elisa |
| Carola | Elisabetta |
| Carolina | Ella |
| Cassandra | Elsa |
| Catena | Elvia |
| Caterina | Elvira |
| Cecilia | Emanuela |
| Celeste | Emilia |
| Cesarina | Emma |
| Chiara | Enrica |
| Ciara | Eriza |
| Cinzia | Ermenegilda |
| Cirilla | Ernesta |
| Clara | Eva |
| Claudia | Fabiana |
| Cora | Fabiola |
| Corinna | Fabrizia |

| | |
|---|---|
| Fausta | Irmina |
| Federica | Isa |
| Fedra | Isabella |
| Felicita | Isidora |
| Ferdinanda | Isotta |
| Filiberta | Iva |
| Filippa | Ivana |
| Fiore | Lara |
| Fiorenze | Lavinia |
| Fioretta | Lea |
| Flavia | Leda |
| Fosca | Leila |
| Franca | Lelia |
| Francesca | Leonida |
| Francine | Letizia |
| Frida | Letteria |
| Gabriella | Lia |
| Gemma | Libera |
| Geraldina | Licia |
| Giada | Lidia |
| Gianna | Liliana |
| Gilda | Lina |
| Gina | Linda |
| Ginevra | Livia |
| Giorgia | Lorena |
| Giovanna | Lorenza |
| Giselda | Lorna |
| Gisella | Luana |
| Giselle | Lucia |
| Gloria | Luciana |
| Grazia | Lucilla |
| Graziella | Lucrezia |
| Greta | Luigia |
| Guendalina | Luisa |
| Ida | Luisella |
| Ileana | Maddalena |
| Imelda | Maia |
| Ines | Manuela |
| Irene | Mara |
| Irma | Marcella |

Mareta
Maria
Marianna
Marina
Marisa
Marta
Martina
Marzia
Matilde
Melissa
Michela
Michelina
Miranda
Mirella
Miriam
Morgana
Nadia
Natalia
Natascia
Neera
Nella
Nicoletta
Nora
Norma
Novella
Odetta
Olga
Ortensia
Palmira
Paola
Penelope
Petronilla
Pia
Priscilla
Regina
Renata
Rina
Rita
Roberta
Robina

Romilda
Romola
Rosalia
Rosanna
Rosaria
Rosetta
Rosina
Rosita
Rossana
Rufina
Sabina
Sabrina
Sandra
Santa
Santina
Sara
Selena
Serena
Silvana
Silvia
Simona
Sofia
Stefania
Susanna
Tamara
Teresa
Tiziana
Tullia
Vala
Valentina
Vanna
Vera
Veronica
Viola
Violanda
Violetta
Virginia
Vittoria
Viviana
Wanda

# 14. Spanish names

## Boys

Abejundio
Agustin
Alarico
Alejandro
Alfonso
Alonso
Alvaro
Amador
Amato
Amistad
Antonio
Armando
Carlos
Castel
Caton
Celio
Chale
Cid
Claudio
Cornelio
Cortes
Cristo
Cruze
Darien
Demetrius
Desidirio
Devante
Diego
Efrain
Emilio
Enrique
Esteban
Fausto
Federico
Felipe
Ferdinando

Fernando
Francisco
Galeno
Gambero
Garcia
Gentil
Gomez
Guillermo
Hernando
Iago
Isidro
Jaguar
Javier
Jeremias
Jorge
Jose
Juan
Leonardo
Lucio
Luis
Manuel
Marco
Miguel
Natal
Navarro
Neron
Nevada
Orlando
Othello
Oziel
Pablo
Pacifico
Pancho
Paolo
Pedro
Pepe

Rafael
Ramiro
Ramon
Renaldo
Rico
Roderigo
Rodolfo
Rodrigo
Rogelio
Salado
Salvador
Sancho
Santiago
Santos
Senon
Seville
Tajo
Tomas
Vittorio
Xavier
Zavier

## Girls

Adoncia
Alatea
Aldonza
Alejandra
Alita
Allegra
Amata
Belicia
Belita
Bonita
Buena
Carmelita
Carmen
Catalina
Chiquita
Cochiti

Coco
Consuelo
Corazon
Cortesia
Delma
Delores
Dolores
Dominga
Dorota
Drina
Duena
Eldora
Elvira
Engracia
Enrica
Esmeralda
Esperanza
Ester
Felipa
Fidelia
Francisca
Galaxia
Gitana
Hermosa
Imelda
Isabel
Isleta
Jaimica
Jaira
Juana
Juanita
Karlotta
Kesare
Latoya
Liani
Lona
Lourdes
Lucetta
Lucia

Luigia
Lujuana
Lynda
Madra

Manuela
Maribel
Mariposa
Mariquita
Marita
Marta
Melisenda
Melosa
Mercedes
Mireya
Mora
Neva
Nevada
Numa
Olalla
Olino
Pacifica
Paloma
Patia
Pepa
Pepita

Perla
Pilar
Ria
Rica
Rosario
Rosita
Salvadora
Sandia
Savanna
Sevilla
Socorro
Solana
Tia
Tierra
Tulia
Ventura
Vina
Vittoria
Xaviera
Xiomara
Xuxa
Xylia
Yomaris
Ysobel
Zafiro

# 15. Russian names

## Boys

Afanasi
Akim
Alek
Aleksander
Aleksei
Alexei
Andrei
Anisim
Bogdan
Boris
Danil
Dima
Dimitri
Dmitri
Faddei
Fedot
Feofilakt
Feofilart
Ferapont
Foma
Garsah
Gavril
Gennadi
Grigor
Igor
Ilya
Ivan
Karl
Kazimir
Kolya
Luka
Lyov
Mikhail
Mikula
Misha

Nikita
Nikolai
Oleg
Pasha
Pavel
Petya
Radko
Radosalve
Rurik
Sasha
Sergei
Vadim
Vanya
Vasili
Vassilly
Vassily
Viktor
Vitali
Vitya
Vlad
Vladisav
Vladja
Vladmir
Volodya
Volya
Yakim
Yakov
Yaroslav
Yasha
Yuri
Zakhar

## Girls

Agafaya
Aglaya
Agnessa
Akilina
Aksinya
Aleksandra

Aleksandrina
Alyona
Anastasia
Anouska
Antonina
Anushka
Arina
Asya
Ayn
Bogdana
Fedora
Gala
Galina
Galya
Irina
Ivana
Jana
Katinka
Katya
Kenya
Lana
Larisa
Larissa
Lizaveta
Ludmila
Lyuba
Mariya
Mikhaila
Milena

Misha
Nadine
Nadya
Nastasia
Natasha
Polina
Raina
Raya
Roksana
Rula
Sacha
Sasha
Sofiya
Sonya
Stasya
Sveta
Svetlana
Tanya
Tasha
Valeska
Vanna
Vladisalva
Vladmira
Vonda
Yaromira
Yelena
Zhenya
Zina
Zinaida
Zinovia

# 16. Pacific Island names

| Boys | Girls |
|------|-------|
| Ariki | Ema |
| Atiu | Hika |
| Kai | Hiriwa |
| Kauri | Hoku |
| Keanu | Inas |
| Keoni | Kai |
| Kupe | Kaimi |
| Lani | Kalasia |
| Manu | Kalei |
| Marama | Kameli |
| Matareka | Kanani |
| Maui | Kiri |
| Ora | Kohia |
| Oroiti | Kura |
| Rangi | Lani |
| Rata | Mahina |
| Rongo | Maru |
| Tama | Nani |
| Tane | Ora |
| Tangaroa | Rangi |
| Tawhiri | Rewa |
| Tiki | Turua |
| Turi | Ulani |

# 17. American names

## Boys

| | |
|---|---|
| Audey | Fargo |
| Barlow | Hobart |
| Booker | Houston |
| Boone | Jaycee |
| Bradley | Jazz |
| Brando | Jefferson |
| Brant | Jerral |
| Bubba | Jonte |
| Buck | Jorell |
| Butch | Kacy |
| Calhoun | Kale |
| Carson | Kyzer |
| Chance | Lynshawn |
| Chaz | Maverick |
| Chuck | Money |
| Clay | Newbie |
| Clayton | Ox |
| Cobain | Perry |
| Dadrian | Sparky |
| Dakota | Texas |
| Darrick | Tipple |
| Davon | Trey |
| Dewey | Tyonne |
| Dirk | Van |
| Duke | Xen |
| Durand | Xyle |
| Dwight | Yadon |
| Eli | Yancy |
| Emmett | Zaie |
| Everley | Zain |

# Girls

| | |
|---|---|
| Annisa | Kady |
| Arlene | Kalisa |
| Arlinda | Kenna |
| Babe | Kiana |
| Beyonce | Kodi |
| Candice | Krystal |
| Cayla | Leona |
| Cody | Lucky |
| Cookie | Macey |
| Cora | Marlene |
| Coretta | McKayla |
| Dakota | Nebraska |
| Deandra | Olaide |
| Dewi | Peppy |
| Dolly | Rabbit |
| Dusty | Richelle |
| Elegy | Ricky |
| Ember | Sea |
| Etenia | Shania |
| Geena | Shawnee |
| Hawlee | Sherilyn |
| Izzy | Shine |
| Jacey | Taffeta |
| Jadelyn | Tibby |
| Jaxine | Toffey |
| Jay | True |
| Jeri | Truly |
| Jessalyn | Velma |
| Jocelyn | Winona |
| Joplin | Yancey |

# 18. Australian names

## Boys

Adoni
Akama
Allambee
Amaroo
Araluen
Balun
Banjora
Bardo
Barega
Barwon
Cobar
Coorain
Daku
Darel
Derain
Dheran
Dorak
Ganan
Gelar
Jarrah
Jerara

Jirra
Kari
Kolet
Koorong
Kulan
Lowan
Maka
Marron
Matari
Monti
Mowan
Nambur
Nardu
Narrah
Nioka
Orad
Pindan
Uwan
Warra
Yarran

# Girls

| | |
|---|---|
| Akala | Jannali |
| Alinga | Jarrah |
| Alkina | Jiba |
| Alkira | Jirra |
| Amarina | Kadee |
| Apanie | Kaiya |
| Araluen | Kala |
| Arika | Kiah |
| Arinya | Kylie |
| Bakana | Orana |
| Barina | Pangari |
| Bega | Pierah |
| Binda | Tallara |
| Camira | Tarana |
| Coorah | Tathra |
| Darri | Tirranna |
| Ekala | Ulla |
| Ellin | Umina |
| Gedala | Yani |
| Ghera | Yara |
| Gulara | Yindi |
| Hanya | |

# 19. African names

## Boys

Abdalla
Abdul
Abedi
Abiola
Afram
Baakir
Babu
Badrani
Bello
Chacha
Chibale
Chimalsi
Daktari
Diallo
Elewa
Eze
Fahim
Farhani
Ghalib
Haamid
Iman
Jaafar
Kofi
Kosey
Maalik
Mandela
Moswen
Muhammed
Naasir
Nanji
Nassor
Odongo
Paki
Rafiki
Rashad

Rasul
Saad
Saeed
Said
Salaam
Senwe
Tahir
Taji
Talib
Ubora
Ulan
Umar
Waitimu
Yohance
Zahir
Zareb
Zuri

## Girls

Aba
Abayomi
Abebi
Abeo
Abla
Adaeze
Adande
Adanma
Adanna
Adanne
Adero
Adjua
Adwin
Adzo
Afam
Afi

| | |
|---|---|
| Agbeko | Kamaria |
| Aidoo | Kamili |
| Akili | Keisha |
| Akuabia | Kia |
| Akuako | Layla |
| Akwate | Lisha |
| Alaba | Maisha |
| Alaezi | Malika |
| Alyetoro | Omesha |
| Ama | Oni |
| Asha | Paka |
| Ayanna | Pulika |
| Baako | Quisha |
| Baba | Rafiya |
| Badu | Raisa |
| Bahati | Ridhaa |
| Benada | Saada |
| Binah | Sabra |
| Binta | Safari |
| Bisa | Shukuma |
| Bunme | Sisi |
| Chiku | Siti |
| Chinue | Tabita |
| Damisi | Talibah |
| Doli | Tamika |
| Efia | Tawia |
| Eshe | Tisha |
| Fadhila | Uzima |
| Ghalyela | Uzuri |
| Gimbya | Wangari |
| Haiba | Winna |
| Halla | Yaa |
| Hamida | Yakini |
| Hanna | Zalika |
| Imena | Zawadi |
| Jalia | Zuwina |

# 20. Celebrity names

## Boys

Adam (Sandler)
Antonio (Banderas)
Ashton (Kucher)
Ben (Affleck, Stiller)
Brad (Pitt)
Daniel (Radcliffe)
David (Beckham)
Ewan (McGregor)
George (Clooney)
Heath (Ledger)
Jake (Gyllenhall)
Johnny (Depp, Lee Miller)
Jude (Law)
Justin (Timberlake)
Matt (Damon, LeBlanc)
Orlando (Bloom)
Russell (Crowe)
Tom (Cruise, Hanks)

## Girls

Angelina (Jolie)
Beyonce (Knowles)
Cameron (Diaz)
Catherine (Zeta Jones)
Charlize (Theron)
Courtney (Cox-Arquette, Love)
Drew (Barrymore)
Gisele (Bundchen)
Halle (Berry)
Jennifer (Aniston, Lopez)
Julia (Roberts)
Kate (Moss)

Keira (Knightley)
Kylie (Minogue)
Liv (Tyler)
Nicole (Kidman)
Paris (Hilton)
Penelope (Cruz)
Reese (Witherspoon)
Renee (Zelwegger)
Sienna (Miller)
Scarlett (Johanssen)
Uma (Thurman)
Victoria (Beckham)

# 21. Names celebrities give their children

## Boys

| | |
|---|---|
| Aurelius Cy | (Elle McPherson and Arpad Busson) |
| Blanket | (Michael Jackson) |
| Brooklyn | (David and Victoria Beckham) |
| Diezel Ky | (Toni Braxton and Keri Lewis) |
| Giacomo | (Sting and Trudi Styler) |
| Griffin | (Brendan Fraser and Afton Smith) |
| Hopper | (Sean Penn and Robin Wright) |
| Jermajesty | (Jermaine Jackson) |
| Kyd | (David Duchovny and Tea Leoni) |
| Lennon | (Patsy Kensit and Liam Gallagher) |
| Maddox | (Angelina Jolie) |
| Memphis | (Bono) |
| Moses | (Gwyneth Paltrow and Chris Martin) |
| Rafferty | (Jude Law and Sadie Frost) |
| Rocco | (Guy Ritchie and Madonna) |
| Romeo | (David and Victoria Beckham) |
| Ryder | (Kate Hudson) |
| Satchel | (Woody Allen and Mia Farrow) |
| Sindri | (Björk) |
| Zowie | (David Bowie and Iman) |

## Girls

| | |
|---|---|
| Apple | (Gwyneth Paltrow and Chris Martin) |
| Bluebell | (Geri Halliwell) |
| Calico | (Alice and Sheryl Cooper) |
| Fifi Trixibelle | (Paula Yates and Bob Geldof) |
| Fuschia | (Sting and Frances Tomelty) |
| Ireland | (Alec Baldwin and Kim Basinger) |
| Luna Coco | (Frank Lampard and Elen Rive) |
| Peaches | (Paula Yates and Bob Geldof) |
| Pixie | (Paula Yates and Bob Geldof) |
| Princess Tiaamii | (Katie Price and Peter Andre) |
| Poppy Honey | (Jamie and Jules Oliver) |
| Saffron Sahara | (Simon and Yasmin LeBon) |
| Scout | (Demi Moore and Bruce Willis) |
| Sonora | (Alice and Sheryl Cooper) |
| Tigerlily | (Paula Yates and Michael Hutchence) |
| Willow | (Will Smith and Jada Pinkett-Smith) |
| Zola | (Eddie Murphy and Nicole Mitchell) |

# 22. Names derived from literature

## Boys

| | |
|---|---|
| Aragorn | *Lord of the Rings* by J. R. R. Tolkien |
| Aramis | *The Three Musketeers* by Alexandre Dumas |
| Caspian | *Prince Caspian* by C. S. Lewis |
| Cassio | *Othello* by William Shakespeare |
| Darcy | *Pride and Prejudice* by Jane Austin |
| Dorian | *The Picture of Dorian Gray* by Oscar Wilde |
| Hamlet | *Hamlet* by William Shakespeare |
| Iago | *Othello* by William Shakespeare |
| Jem | *To Kill a Mockingbird* by Harper Lee, *Jamaica Inn* by Daphne DuMaurier |
| Lestat | *Vampire Chronicles* by Anne Rice |
| Oberon | *A Midsummer Night's Dream* by William Shakespeare |
| Sawyer | *The Adventures of Tom Sawyer* by Mark Twain |
| Sherlock | *Adventures of Sherlock Holmes* by Sir Arthur Conan Doyle |
| Sinbad | *The Book of 1001 Arabian Nights* |
| Yorick | *Hamlet* by William Shakespeare |

## Girls

| | |
|---|---|
| Arwen | *Lord of the Rings* by J. R. R. Tolkien |
| Belphoebe | *The Fairie Queen* by Edmund Spenser |
| Calypso | *Odyssey* by Homer |
| Dulcinea | *Don Quixote* by Miguel de Cervantes |
| Eowyn | *Lord of the Rings* by J. R. R. Tolkien |
| Eponin | *Les Miserables* by Victor Hugo |
| Galadriel | *Lord of the Rings* by J. R. R. Tolkien |
| Gyneth | *The Bridal of Triermain* by Sir Walter Scott |
| Idril | *The Silmarillion* by J. R. R. Tolkien |
| Jessica | *The Merchant of Venice* by Shakespeare |
| Miranda | *The Tempest* by William Shakespeare |
| Orinthia | *The Apple Cart* by George Bernard Shaw |
| Wendy | *Peter Pan* by J. M. Barrie |

# 23. Names that come from place names

## Boys

Aberdeen
Aleppo
America
Arizona
Arran
Austell
Avon
Babylon
Barrington
Boston
Bramwell
Brecon
Brighton
Brooklyn
Cairo
Carlyle
Creighton
Darby
Denver
Devon
Java
Kent
Lincoln
London
Lyon
Milan
Montana
Powys
Rhodes
Roman
Timor
Tyrol
Utah
Vegas
Warwick
Windsor
Wyndham
York
Yukon
Yuma
Zaire

## Girls

Africa
Atlanta
Cairo
Camden
Capri
China
Daytona
Devon
Devona
Egypt
Florence
Havana
India
Indiana
Ireland
Jamaica
Lamorna
Malaya
Medora
Montana
Orissa
Persia
Petra
Rhonda
Savannah
Skye
Sydney
Tennessee
Turin
Tyne
Valletta
Venice
Verona
Zennor

# 24. Timeless names

## Boys

Alexander
Andrew
Daniel
David
Edward
James
John
Mark
Matthew
Michael
Nicholas
Peter
Robert
Simon
Thomas
William

## Girls

Alison
Anne
Catherine
Claire
Elizabeth
Emma
Jane
Joanna
Julia
Laura
Maria
Rachel
Rebecca
Sarah
Victoria

# 25. Names that will date

## Boys

Brooklyn
Cade
Cruz
Heath
Jayden
Joshua
Leonardo
Mackenzie
Noah
Orlando
Preston
Shayne
Tyler
Unique
Zane

## Girls

Britney
Chanelle
Halle
Keira
Kylie
Jordan
Molly
Paris
Peaches
Poppy
Ruby
Scarlett
Unique

# 26. Names from the heavens

## Boys

Arcturus
Aries
Caelum
Castor
Dorado
Draco
Leo
Lupus
Orion
Polaris
Regulus
Saggitarius
Scorpio
Sirius
Taurus

## Girls

Adharis
Aquarius
Auriga
Carina
Cygnus
Deneb
Gemini
Libra
Lyra
Pisces
Ursa
Vega
Virgo

# 27. Names for babies who'll change the world

## Boys

Abraham (Lincoln)
Churchill (Winston)
Ghandi (Mahatma)
Henry (Kissinger)
Kennedy (John F.)
Kofi (Anan)
Lennon (John)
Lincoln (Abraham)
Luther (Martin Luther King)
Mahatma (Ghandi)
Mandela (Nelson)
Martin (Luther King)
Nelson (Mandela)
Winston (Churchill)

## Girls

Anne (Frank)
Diana (Princess Diana)
Eleanor (Roosevelt)
Elizabeth (Queen Elizabeth)
Emmeline (Pankhurst)
Emily (Dickinson)
Florence (Nightingale)
Helen (Kelly)
Joan (of Arc)
Marie (Curie)
Mary (Seacole)
Oprah (Winfrey)
Rosa (Parks)
Teresa (Mother Teresa)
Victoria (Queen Victoria)

# 28. Names for future millionaires

## Boys

Alan
Aristo
Aston
Bill
Blake
Branson
Carrington
Cash
Colby
Donald
Ferrari
Richard
Stelios
Ulrich

## Girls

Alexis
Elodie
Etenia
Ivana
Jemima
Mercedes
Money
Olivia
Paris
Porsche
Richelle
Soraya
Sugar
Tamara
Tara
Ulrika

# 29. Names for future scientists

## Boys

Albert
Archimedes
Darwin
Franklin
Gallileo
Isaac
Leonardo
Michael
Nicholas
Niels
Thomas

## Girls

Alberta
Amalie
Dian
Elizabeth
Hypatia
Jewel
Marie
Rachel
Trotula
Virginia

# 30. Names that will help your child be popular

## Boys

Adam
Bradley
Brett
Callum
Cody
Drew
Ethan
Finlay
Harry
Heath
Joe
Nick
Stephen
Tom

## Girls

Amber
Amy
Ashley
Charlie
Daisy
Darcy
Emma
Jenny
Lauren
Lucy
Madison
Sophie

# 31. Names for future artists

## Boys

Adelfredo
Anton
Bailey
Benton
Blaine
Cameron
Claude
Cosmo
Dai
Drew
Firenze
Giovanni
Hermes
Hockney
Kent
Jackson
Jared
Joachim
Leonardo
Luc
Lyndon
Michelangelo
Ortensio
Pablo
Pavel
Raphael
Remington
Renoir
Romano
Salvador
Umber
Vincent

## Girls

Arwyn
Callidora
Cezanne
Chante
Charis
Cistine
Florence
Frida
Galena
Georgia
Kaethe
Karlotta
Marianne
Ophelia
Psyche
Rafaella
Siena
Sonia
Tallulah
Thalia
Zaina

# 32. Names for future writers

## Boys

Amis
Austen
Blake
Byron
Cohen
Conrad
Cooper
Dahl
Dylan
Eliot
Emerson
Fable
Fitzgerald
Hugo
Lewis
Milton
Murdoch
Roald
William
Wordsworth

## Girls

Anais
Angelou
Carroll
Charlotte
Brontë
Dante
Fay
Harper
Iris
Joyce
Lovelace
Malory
Shelley
Tennessee
Virginia
Zadie

# 33. Names for sporty types

## Boys

Bjorn
Boris
David
George
Greg
Jesse
Joe
Lance
Lennox
Lyndon
Magic
Nick
Pele
Rio
Sebastian
Sugar Ray
Tiger
Tyson

## Girls

Anjanette
Annika
Babe
Chris
Dara
Fatima
Kelly
Martina
Nadia
Paula
Sally
Serena
Tessa
Venus
Wilma
Zola

# 34. Macho names

Ace
Al
Arnie
Butch
Cal
Cane
Dolph
Duke
Jock
Mack
Rebel
Ripley
Rocco
Rock
Spike
Vinnie

# 35. Girlie names

Babe
Bibi
Cherry
Daisy
Dolly
Fifi
Honey
Kitten
Lulu
Milly
Petal
Pink
Pixie
Primrose
Sissy
Sugar
Sweetie
Trixie

# 36. Old-fashioned names that are cool again

## Boys

Alfie
Archie
Barney
Freddie
George
Harry
Henry
Isaac
Levi
Oscar
Reuben
Rupert
Sebastian
Theo
Zachary

## Girls

Ada
Alma
Betty
Dora
Grace
Flora
Florence
Harriet
Mabel
Maisie
Martha
May
Milly
Molly
Olivia
Pearl
Ruby

# 37. Regal names

## Boys

Charles
Edmund
Edward
George
Harry
Henry
James
John
Richard
William

## Girls

Alexandra
Anne
Caroline
Diana
Elizabeth
Margaret
Mary
Victoria
Zara

# 38. Unisex names

Aidan
Alex
Andy
Ashley
Bailey
Billie
Blaine
Bobby
Brooke
Bryn
Cal
Cary
Casey
Chris
Corey
Courtney
Devon
Drew
Erin
Evelyn
Frankie
Gabriel
Georgie
Glen
Hilary
Jackie
Jaime
Jayden
Jesse
Jordan
Jules

Kay
Kelly
Kim
Kit
Lee
Lesley
Leslie
Lyndsay
Lysander
Micky
Nat
Nicky
Paris
Pat
Randy
René
Robin
Sam
Sandy
Sean
Shane
Shannon
Shauny
Shelby
Shelley
Stevie
Taylor
Terry
Toby
Tony
Valentine
Vic

# 39. Names inspired by colours

## Boys

Blue
Bronze
Brown
Cobalt
Goldie
Hessian
Indigo
Jasper
Jet
Lemony
Minty
Ochre
Red
Silver
Slater
Umber

## Girls

Amber
Azure
Bianca
Cerise
Cerulean
Chartreuse
Coral
Cyan
Damask
Emerald
Goldie
Indigo
Ivory
Jade
Lavender
Lilac
Magenta
Mauve
Olive
Peach
Pearl
Pink
Plum
Poppy
Primrose
Rose
Ruby
Sapphire
Scarlet
Silver
Violet

# 40. Flower names for girls

Acacia
Alyssa
Amaryllis
Azalea
Begonia
Blossom
Bluebell
Bryony
Camelia
Clover
Crisanta
Dahlia
Daisy
Delphinium
Fleur
Flora
Gardenia
Heather
Hyacinth
Ianthe
Iris
Jacaranda
Jasmine
Jolan
Joquil

Lilac
Lillian
Lily
Lotus
Krysanthe
Margeurite
Marigold
Myrtle
Narcissus
Neroli
Oleander
Pansy
Petula
Petunia
Poppy
Primrose
Rosa
Rose
Rosemary
Snowdrop
Tulip
Violante
Violet
Yasmin
Yolanda

# 41. Names for bad boys and girls

## Boys

Billy
Bones
Bruno
Byron
Heathcliff
Kid
Marlon
Mick
Ripper
Romeo
Scorpion
Sonny
Vinnie

## Girls

Bellatrix
Bonnie
Carmilla
Circe
Delilah
Eve
Gilda
Jezebel
Lilith
Lola
Nikita
Salome
Scarlett
Siren
Tallulah

# 42. Names inspired by moods

## Boys

Ardent
Brave
Calm
Fierce
Gallant
Grim
Loyal
Rage
Storm
Sunny
Valiant

## Girls

Bliss
Blythe
Constance
Delight
Desire
Ecstasy
Euphoria
Gay
Happy
Jolly
Joy
Patience
Peace
Serenity
Sincerity

# 43. Spiritual names

## Boys

Angelo
Avalon
Free
Hevan
Idol
Nirvana
Pax
Soul
Spirit
Star
Truth
Utope

## Girls

Angel
Bliss
Deity
Destiny
Divine
Dream
Elysia
Harmony
Heaven
Infinity
Paradise
Serendipity
Sky

# 44. Names with songs dedicated to them

## Boys

| | |
|---|---|
| Al | It's what Paul Simon wished to be called in 1986 |
| Alfie | Theme from the Michael Caine film by Cilla Black in 1966 |
| Angelo | Brotherhood of Man chart-topper |
| Ben | From 1972 by Michael Jackson |
| Billy | Paper Lace urged him not to be a hero |
| Brian | Title track to Monty Python's *Life of Brian*, 1979 |
| Curly | A No.12 hit for the Move in 1968 |
| Cyril | Nice one for Cockerel Chorus and other football fans |
| Daniel | Elton John song about a blind brother |
| Denis | Blondie's first big hit, 1978 |
| Ernie | Benny Hill's milkman |
| Fernando | Abba's wartime hero |
| Figaro | Another Brotherhood of Man favourite |
| Frankie | Do you remember this Sister Sledge 1984 chart topper? |
| Geno | Who-oh-oh oh-oh |
| Jimmy | A poor little fella according to the Undertones |
| Johnny | Perhaps the most frequently used male name in pop |
| Louie | Louie Louie is often voted the greatest single ever |
| Luka | Suzanne Vega's friend in the mid 1980s |
| Mickey | Toni Basil's pretty man never did understand |
| Nigel | XTC were making plans for him in 1980 |
| Rasputin | That lover of the Russian queen |
| Robin | He was rockin' for Michael Jackson in the 1970s |
| Stan | Eminem's 2000 stalking girlfriend-killing fan |
| Vincent | This Don McLean track is a tribute to Van Gogh |

## Girls

| | |
|---|---|
| Alison | Elvis Costello song |
| Angelina | A Louis Prima classic, rather than the ballerina |
| Angie | 1973 Rolling Stones' hit, also 'Angie Baby' by Helen Reddy |
| Annie | 'Annie's Song' by John Denver |
| Babooshka | Kate Bush's 1980 ode to a mistrusting wife |
| Barbara Ann | As in Bar-bar-bar bar... by the Beach Boys |
| Bernadette | Four Tops hit |
| Billie Jean | ...Was not Jacko's love in his 1983 hit |
| Brandy | Scott English's 1972 original before it became 'Mandy' |
| Carol | Oh this was a big hit for Neil Sedaka |
| Caroline | Status Quo's 1973 name of choice |
| Carrie | She doesn't live with Cliff Richard anymore |
| Carrie-Anne | The Hollies wondered what her game was in the 1960s |
| Cecilia | Simon and Garfunkel song, made a hit by Suggs in 1996 |
| Charlotte | Anne – A minor hit for Julian Cope |
| Chiquitita | Abba wanted to know what was wrong in 1979 |
| Clair | First of two chart-toppers for Gilbert O'Sullivan |
| Claudette | Early Everly Brothers No.1, 1958 |
| Delilah | A spurned Tom Jones gives his lover what for |
| Diana | Paul Anka, 1957 and Michael Jackson in 1988 |
| Diane | The Bachelors, 1964 |
| Donna | Marty Wilde and Ritchie Valens in 1959 |
| Eileen | Come on – it's Dexy's Midnight Runners |
| Elenore | A hit by The Turtles |
| Eloise | Barry Ryan in 1968 then the Damned in 1986 |
| Elona | As in Elona Gay, OMD, 1980 |
| Emma | Hot Chocolate sang about her in 1973 |
| Georgy | As in Hey there, Georgy Girl (The Seekers, 1968) |
| Gloria | Van Morrison or U2 |
| Iris | Late 1990s Goo Goo Dolls hit |

| | |
|---|---|
| Ivy | The Coasters thought she was poison in 1959 |
| Jacqueline | A 2007 hit for the Coral |
| Janie | Janie Got A Gun |
| Jean | Jean Genie is perhaps the best use of this |
| Joanna | Kool and the Gang hit |
| Jolene | The woman who made Dolly Parton jealous! |
| Julie | Oh Julie, by Shakin' Stevens |
| Julia | Hit by Chris Rea |
| Kayleigh | Massive hit for Marillion, 1985 |
| Kyrie | Mr Mister, 1986 |
| Laura | A Scissor Sisters song, and also a hit for Ricky Valence |
| Layla | An excuse to play air guitar at the christening? |
| Lola | A Kinks classic |
| Louise | The Human league wished they were still lovers in 1984 |
| Lucille | She don't do her Daddy's will |
| Lyla | A 2005 chart topper for Oasis |
| Maggie | A hit for Rod Stewart whilst Honeybus couldn't let her go |
| Mandy | Barry Manilow and Westlife have both sung about her |
| Maria | Ricky Martin's breakthrough hit |
| Marie | Another one of Shakin' Steven's ladies |
| Marlene | Who Suzanne Vega saw on the wall in 1986 |
| Mary | The Scissor Sisters and Supergrass sang about her |
| Michelle | A Beatles classic |
| Minnie | As in the Moocher |
| Mona | Craig McLachan's big hit |
| Nelly | The elephant |
| Nikita | Elton John fell for this Russian name back in 1985 |
| Pamela | So lovely, Wayne Fontana sang about her twice |
| Peggy Sue | Buddy Holly certainly knew her |
| Rhiannon | A Fleetwood Mac minor hit |
| Roni | Bobby Brown's favourite name before Whitney? |
| Rosalie | Brotherhood of Man thought this one was sweet |
| Rosanna | Toto, 1983 |

| | |
|---|---|
| Rose-Marie | Back in the 1950s, this was a hit for Slim Whitman |
| Roxanne | It's by the Police and about a prostitute |
| Ruby | Hits for the Kaiser Chiefs and Kenny Rogers |
| Sandy | John Travolta's ballad in *Grease* |
| Sara | A soft rock anthem from Starship, 1986 |
| Sherry | A name for the Four Seasons |
| Sue | As in Runaround Sue |
| Susie | Wake Up Little Susie |
| Tammy | A hit by Debbie Reynolds |
| Valerie | Steve Winwood's 1980s anthem and the Zutons, 2006 |
| Veronica | Elvis Costello's tribute to his gran |
| Wendy | Early Beach Boys hit |

# 45. Nasty nickname-prone names

## Boys

Adolf
Billy
Buck
Farley
Hank
Jesse
Kelly
Titus
Will

## Girls

Coco
Daphne
Ellie
Gay
Kelly
Lesbia
Porsche
Priscilla
Rhea
Tess

# 46. Playground-proof names

## Boys

Adam
Andrew
Ben
Carl
David
Jack
James
John
Lee
Mark
Michael
Stephen
Thomas

## Girls

Amy
Catherine
Charlotte
Chloe
Emma
Jenny
Kate
Lucy
Rachel
Rebecca
Sarah
Sophie
Zoë

# 47. Names of patron saints

## Boys

| | |
|---|---|
| Andrew | *Scotland* |
| Christopher | *travellers* |
| Clement | *stonecutters* |
| David | *Wales* |
| Domin | *astronomers, scientists* |
| Frances | *animal welfare* |
| George | *England* |
| James | *vets* |
| John | *tanners* |
| Jude | *desperate situations* |
| Luke | *doctors* |
| Martin | *soldiers* |
| Matthew | *accountants* |
| Nicholas | *charity, children, prisoners, bakers* |
| Patrick | *Ireland* |
| Peter | *fishermen* |
| Sebastian | *athletes* |
| Valentine | *lovers* |

## Girls

| | |
|---|---|
| Agatha | *nurses* |
| Anne | *equestrians* |
| Barbara | *architects, builders* |
| Bernadette | *shepherds* |
| Catherine | *preachers, philosophers* |
| Cecilia | *musicians* |
| Joan | *soldiers* |
| Margaret | *nurses* |
| Martha | *cooks* |
| Monica | *wives, survivors of domestic violence* |
| Rita | *impossible situations* |
| Zita | *domestic servants, maids* |

# 48. Names inspired by nature

## Boys

Acorn
Ash
Breeze
Cliff
Cyclone
Fire
Forest
Hail
Heath
Hurricane
Ice
Rocky
Rowan
Smokey
Storm
Tor
Vernon
Woody

## Girls

Apple
Autumn
Berry
Blossom
Bramble
Brooke
Cirrus
Cloud
Crystal
Dandelion
Dawn
Dusk
Eartha
Fen
Fern
Flower
Gaia
Leaf
Luna
Moon
Ocean
Pebbles
Petal
Rain
Raindrop
Ripple
Shamrock
Sky
Snow
Snowflake
Spring
Summer
Sunset
Sunshine

# 49. Names you can't shorten

## Boys

Al
Ben
Bill
Bob
Brett
Bryn
Cade
Cal
Dave
Ed
Fred
Gil
Giles
Hal
Hugh
Jack
Jake
Joe
John
Keith
Ken
Lars
Mick
Mike
Nick
Pat
Pete
Ray
Rob
Ron
Sam
Sol
Tim
Tom
Vic

Will
Yan
Zac

## Girls

Anne
Babs
Bo
Brie
Cath
Drew
Gayle
Gwen
Jo
Kaede
Kate
Kim
Mo
Pam
Pat
Sian
Sue
Trish
Val
Wynne

# 50. Names from mythology

## Boys

Achilles
Adonis
Ambrose
Apollo
Damian
Hercules
Jason
Mark
Martin
Paris
Sirius
Thor
Zeus

## Girls

Aurora
Calypso
Cassandra
Cynthia
Daphne
Denise
Helen
Hera
Iris
Leda
Martina
Minerva
Narcissa
Penelope
Phoebe
Sybil
Venus

# 51. Names which are foreign words

## Boys

| | |
|---|---|
| Allegro | Happy (Italian) |
| Amigo | Friend (Spanish) |
| Amor | Love (Spanish) |
| Cade | Juniper (French) |
| Dimanche | Sunday (French) |
| Domingo | Sunday (Spanish) |
| Herbe | Grass (French) |
| Fiero | Proud (Italian) |
| Garcon | Boy (French) |
| Firenze | Florence (Italian) |
| Jubilo | Joy (Spanish) |
| Soleil | Sun (French) |
| Tierno | Tender (Spanish) |
| Vida | Life (Spanish) |
| Vrai | True (French) |

## Girls

| | |
|---|---|
| Alea | Chance (Italian) |
| Aria | Air (Italian) |
| Carina | Cute (Italian) |
| Carita | Charity (Italian) |
| Jolie | Pretty (French) |
| Juedi | Tuesday (French) |
| Mai | May (French) |
| Musique | Music (French) |
| Neve | Snow (Spanish) |
| Ora | Hour (Italian) |
| Perla | Pearl (Spanish, Italian) |
| Satine | Satin (French) |
| Tia | Aunt (Spanish) |
| Valletta | Little valley (Italian) |

conclusion

Whether you have set your heart on the name you now instinctively know is right for your child, or you now have several potential choices on your shortlist, this book will hopefully have helped you get closer to finding your child's name.

Just remember, whatever your final choice, the way you feel about the name you choose for your baby will change immeasurably as your child makes this name his or her own, and infuses it with all the quirks, strengths and flaws that make up their personality.

Regardless of how many namesakes you meet in your life, or how many 'better' names you come across after you've signed the birth certificate, the name you find now will always, for you at least, be theirs and as such, it's a word you will always love. Good luck!

taking it further

## History of names

The meaning and origins of names in this book are given as those most commonly agreed upon. However, many names have complex origins and experts sometimes argue about the true meaning of names. If you would like to learn more about the history and linguistic origins of names you love, *The Oxford Dictionary of First Names* (Oxford University Press) is a useful reference. Helpful websites include **www.thinkbabynames.com** and **www.behindthename.com**.

## The psychology of names

How names affect the way we think, behave and connect and the psychological impression that certain names tend to have on others is an area that's attracted a great deal of in-depth study in recent years. Some of the most interesting studies have been carried out by Professor Albert Mehrabian at the University of California. To read more about the psychology of names see his books *The Name Game* (Penguin) and *The Baby Name Report Card* (Penguin).

## Registering your baby's name

To find out more about who can register a baby's name and the rules that apply for your part of the country visit the General Register Office website at **www.gro.gov.uk** or contact them directly by letter, phone or email:

Births & Deaths Section
Room D209
General Register Office
Trafalgar Road
SOUTHPORT
PR8 2HH
Tel: +44 (0) 151 471 4805 (9 a.m. to 5 p.m. Monday to Friday)
Email: **registering.births@ons.gsi.gov.uk**

# Changing your baby's name

If you wish to change your baby's name or if you wish to change your own surname at the time of your baby's birth, you will need to contact one of the registered deed poll services which are able to issue deed poll documents changing your or your baby's name. The biggest of these is the UK Deed Poll service.

UK Deed Poll Service
Freebournes Court,
Witham
CM8 2BL
Tel: 0800 4488484
Website: **www.ukdps.co.uk**

# Baby naming trends

To find out which names are currently the most popular in the UK and to see archive lists of the most popular names, contact the Office of National Statistics, who publish lists of the top 100 names for boys and girls each year and who make some historical lists available.

Office for National Statistics
Customer Contact Centre
Room 1.015
Office for National Statistics
Cardiff Road
Newport
NP10 8XG
Tel: (0) 845 601 3034
Email: **info@statistics.gov.uk**. (Please include a contact telephone number and postal address)
Website: **www.statistics.gov.uk**

teach
yourself

**positive pregnancy**
denise tiran

- Do you want a healthy and happy pregnancy?
- Would you like to know what to expect in these amazing nine months?
- Do you need practical advice and a sympathetic approach?

**Positive Pregnancy** gives inspirational advice to help you make the most of this exciting new time in your life. It covers your practical, emotional and physical needs before, during and after pregnancy, helping you feel confident and in control. From birth options to feeding choices and returning to work, it is full of sensible, reassuring support.

**Denise Tiran** is an experienced midwife and Director of Expectancy Ltd. She is a visiting lecturer at the University of Greenwich, writes widely for the national press and is a published author.

**teach yourself**

# yoga for pregnancy & birth
uma dinsmore-tulli

- Do you want to be relaxed and well in your pregnancy?
- Would you like to learn how breathing can help during labour?
- Would you like yoga techniques to keep you healthy after birth?

**Yoga for Pregnancy and Birth** shows you how yoga and breath work can keep you relaxed and healthy during and after your pregnancy. It has simple exercises to practise at home, with plenty of emotional support and spiritual insight, and a CD which shows you how breathing can help reduce labour pain and keep you calm.

**Uma Dinsmore-Tulli** is a yoga therapist, writer, lecturer and trainer who first learnt yoga when she was four years old and has been teaching yoga since 1994.